FEED THE HUNGRY

FEED THE HUNGRY

How to Set Up and Run a Successful Meal Program

Shannah Pogline

IGUANA

Copyright © 2023 Shannah Pogline
Published by Iguana Books
720 Bathurst Street, Suite 410
Toronto, ON M5S 2R4

Publisher: Meghan Behse
Editor: Anne Brennan
Front cover design: Jonathan Relph
Front cover models (from bottom to top): Conner Henry, Génesis Vázquez, Michelle Villalobos, Steven Zehm, Stephen Pogline, Nahum Vázquez and photography director Sandy Mercado

ISBN 978-1-77180-592-6 (paperback)
ISBN 978-1-77180-591-9 (epub)

This is an original print edition of *Feed the Hungry: How to Set Up and Run a Successful Meal Program*.

Table of Contents

Chapter 1

Why Set Up a Meal Program?

In 2013, I was president of the Parent Advisory Council (PAC) at my kids' elementary school. To help boost morale, we decided to offer a free hot lunch to every child in the school. A local grocery chain donated hot dogs, buns, condiments, apples, and juice boxes, and helped serve the meal.

Several parents tearfully thanked the principal for providing this meal at no charge, because they couldn't afford to give their kids money for the hot lunches offered by the school once a month.

When I heard that, I was shocked. We live in an area filled with beautiful homes and new vehicles. There's a recreational vehicle in every other driveway. We see lots of busy people wearing stylish clothes. What we don't see are all the families in need living in basement suites. I was stunned to realize that in our upscale area, in small corners of those nice homes, low-income families were struggling to make ends meet.

I thought about this after the lunch as I made my way to the school gym to hear a folk band give an afternoon concert. The children entered the gym and took their places quietly, listening attentively to their instructions. There was a calm energy in the room as the musicians told the kids when to clap and how to participate. I idly wondered why there was none of the excited, rambunctious behaviour we typically saw. The children were completely engaged. Other assemblies weren't like this one!

Then it hit me: every child in that room had been fed. My eyes filled with tears.

Seeing a Difference

Struggling families sometimes have trouble getting enough to eat.

I spent sixteen years as a professional chef. I fed people—it's what I'm wired to do. I've cooked for fine-dining restaurants, pubs, golf courses, manufacturing plants, seniors' homes, catering companies, institutions, nonprofit organizations, film companies, and schools. I know about both the culinary aspects and the business side of feeding people.

So I started crunching numbers, to see how I could help these hungry kids. I wanted to give them a good meal every day so they'd get the nutrition they needed for learning. There were 250 children in our school. Providing each one with a free lunch every day would be a huge expense, but I didn't want to exclude anyone. It wouldn't be fair to make some kids pay while others got lunch for free. And I didn't want to expose the less-well-off kids to potential ridicule from their peers.

Breakfast, though—breakfast was doable. So I called around, raised money, applied for grants, worked with the school principal to install a kitchen, and started a daily breakfast program. It took less than a year. I set up a five-week menu plan that included ham-and-cheese melts with apple slices and milk . . . whole-wheat cinnamon buns . . . zucchini bake sweetened with apple sauce . . . Shrek smoothies (made with kale, strawberries, milk, yogurt, and a little honey) with granola bars . . . pancakes . . . even hot chocolate made with milk on Fridays, to attract the older kids during cold weather.

Before long, we were providing a daily breakfast for sixty to ninety children—a quarter to a third of the school's population. And we noticed a remarkable change: the principal had virtually no behavioural issues to deal with before recess, and only the occasional problem after recess. Behavioural problems spiked only after lunch.

When she looked at who the problem kids were, she realized some of them weren't getting enough for lunch. So we encouraged them to help themselves to extra food at breakfast and eat it at lunchtime.

Our program was so successful that people from the school district asked me to help set up breakfast programs for at-risk children in other schools. I soon caught the bug. Over the next few years I helped with fundraising, organized volunteers, and created menu plans and recipes for food programs sponsored by schools, churches, food banks, and nonprofit organizations.

As I became known for my expertise with meal programs, people and organizations started asking me for help. They wanted to set up food programs for children, adults, and seniors in their own communities, but didn't know where to begin. They wanted to learn how to source supplies, calculate food costs, create healthy menus, do meal prep, cook for large groups, fundraise, and market their programs.

I looked for a written resource that answered their questions, but couldn't find one. So I decided to write this book and share what I've learned.

Answering the Critics

"Why should I pay to feed someone else? Or someone else's kids? Why can't they just get a job and feed themselves?"

I hear questions like this all the time, and it's disheartening. The truth is that not everyone who needs a food program is a drug addict or a couch potato. Many apparently prosperous folks are, behind closed doors, just one payday away from hardship. There are plenty of reasons someone might need a food program—a lost job, extra medical expenses, a death or divorce, illness, depression, debt.

When people eat properly, they function better. It's as simple as that. They're less disruptive and more successful in the classroom. They're more productive at work. They're healthier, happier, and more involved in their community. So it pays to make sure everyone in your neighbourhood is properly fed.

In addition to nourishment, a food program can provide access to outreach workers, counsellors, and life-skills trainers. This can help get high-risk individuals back on their feet.

Investing a few dollars now can help prevent big expenses later. Transforming a malnourished community into a healthier, more productive one can mean lower costs for health care and policing. It can mean lower unemployment and less crime, which means homes increase in value. When you support a food program, you're not just "shelling out" on "losers" who can't feed themselves — you're benefiting your entire community.

Next time you're really hungry, try to concentrate on something. Note your mood. Are you *hangry*? Not eating can make you hungry and angry. A drop in blood sugar can lower your tolerance and sharpen your temper, making it hard to concentrate and deal with challenging situations. Your judgment isn't at its best. Your quality of life drops.

Now imagine what it must be like to feel this way for most of the day, every day, while people around you expect you to function normally.

Starting a Meal Program

With living expenses constantly rising, it's getting harder and harder for some people to get by. Food banks and food programs are critical for them.

It's not hard to set up a program that provides regular meals for people who are at risk. If you have good organizational skills and know what's required, you can do it. This book tells you everything you need to know to get started and to be successful. It also shows you how to make an existing program more cost-effective and sustainable. We'll talk about assessing your community's needs, choosing the right kind of program, finding facilities and personnel, budgeting, planning meals, ordering supplies, working with distributors, involving other community programs, and more.

One of the big challenges, of course, is fundraising. At this time, Canada is the only G8 country without a national school-based food program. While the American Congress spends approximately $398 million a year just on its summer school food program (2012 figures), Canada provides virtually no government support for meal programs. So it's important that people like you and me look after one another.

As a professional chef, I'm passionate about feeding people. I applaud your desire to help make sure everyone in your community gets enough to eat. My wish is for everyone to have the opportunity to eat a nutritious meal every day.

Chapter 2

What Does Your Community Need?

A number of steps are involved in setting up and running a successful meal program.

First you have to figure out who your clients are and what they need. Then you have to choose the type of program that best meets those needs, find an accessible space with suitable kitchen facilities, recruit staff, create menus, and buy ingredients, all while staying within a budget. And of course you need to find stable funding to support your program.

It sounds like a lot, but it's manageable if you take it a step at a time. This book will take you through the steps, showing you how to succeed and what to avoid. I've created and operated a variety of food programs, and have learned first-hand that it takes careful planning to give a program a solid foundation.

In this chapter, we'll talk about how to identify your clients and design a food program that best meets their needs.

Who Are Your Clients?

Who will your program serve? What do they need?

This topic came up for me when I discovered that some children in our otherwise affluent area weren't getting enough to eat. Kids from low-income families, many living in basement suites, were unable to enjoy the monthly hot lunches offered for a fee by the school. Some kids were coming to school without having breakfast, and some weren't bringing any lunch. Inadequate nourishment was affecting their behaviour and their learning.

I suggested that we set up a free breakfast program, to ensure that every child could start the day well nourished. Kids without lunches could also take something from breakfast to eat at midday. The principal quickly agreed to my proposal. For years she'd known that there was a need for a food program, but she'd had no idea how to start one.

We decided to open the program to every child in the school, as well as to parents, siblings who didn't attend the school, and children from nearby schools. In addition to helping everyone who needed it, this would prevent any stigma from arising, since everyone could use the program equally.

A successful food program reaches every member of the targeted group. It's easy for clients to access, and it doesn't discriminate. If people can't take advantage of your program because of age, disability, gender, sexual orientation, race, ethnicity, or religious or political beliefs, you won't achieve your goals. That's why you must determine ahead of time who your clients are, what they need, and what challenges they may be facing.

To figure out who you want to serve, ask yourself the following questions:

- What does your ideal food program look like?
- Will you serve only the homeless?
- Will you offer free food, or will you provide meals at reduced prices?

- Will you include only families who are struggling financially?
- Will you include only people within a certain income range?
- Will your program be serving a certain age range?
- Do you want to help single parents?
- Will your program be open to everyone, regardless of their positions in life?

Whichever choices you make, you can be proud that you're giving people a chance to have better lives and healthier futures.

What Do They Need?

Each food program is different, because client circumstances and dynamics can vary widely. Do your clients need a program once a week? Every couple of days? Every day? Do they mostly need snacks? Full meals? Morning or evening service? You'll need to answer many questions as you shape your program.

The best type of program is the one that best meets your clients' needs. High school students' circumstances are different from those of elementary kids, and the dynamics of a church-based program are different from those of a program based in a community centre. At-risk kids, for example, might benefit most from a breakfast program, especially if it gives them a safe, warm place to go early in the morning, to get away from unhappy home situations. There's a lot to think about.

You won't be running this program alone, so talk with all of your partners. See what they think is best, and make a unified decision. Having other people influence your choices can be a good thing, because they may think of things you don't.

A breakfast program can provide at-risk kids with a safe place to go earlier in the day. While many schools fund lunches for at-risk children, kids who need lunch probably need breakfast and supper provided, too.

Knowing your community's needs will help you determine what kind of program can best meet them. There are five basic types of meal programs to choose from:

- Grab-and-go meals
- Sit-down meals
- Classroom meals
- Take-home meals
- Catered meals

Grab-and-Go Meals

A grab-and-go program provides meals that clients can pick up in their hands and eat without plates. This type of program is handy if you don't have enough space for a sit-down program. Clients can grab the food and take it with them. Since they don't have to eat it all in one sitting, they can ration it out, reducing their hunger throughout the day.

Meals of this type can be distributed in strategic places. If you put them near the school entrance or in a common area, kiddos who come to school late can grab something quickly and run to class, or grab food between classes. Even though eating in class isn't the best solution, most teachers allow kids to do so nowadays—especially the ones they know are at risk.

A grab-and-go bagged meal is a quick, convenient way to offer food to large groups. Grab-and-go meals generally require little cooking. If you use nonperishable food items, you can prepare the meals off-site the day before and put them in bags. When you bring them to the distribution facility, you can place them on carts for easy pickup.

If your clients can pre-order their bagged meals, you'll know exactly how many meals to make. However, it can be difficult to get pre-orders from some populations, and you will need to find another way to determine the numbers.

You could, for example, pair up with an organization that offers life-skills courses for marginalized people. You could supply their lunches, or send them off with bagged dinners. You could even create your own course and advertise that it includes a meal. If you require pre-registration for the course, you'll know how many meals to prepare.

When I was pregnant with my first son, more than two decades ago, I attended a group that taught pregnancy care to women who were struggling financially. They measured our tummies each week and taught us how to care for our children once they came into the world. I joined the group for the support and information, sure, but the main reason I attended each meeting was for the four-litre milk coupon they gave me each week and the hot lunch they supplied at the meeting. You could use this same idea with bagged meals. Get your clients to come by giving them something they need or want.

Bagged meals must be kept at the proper temperature. Keep perishable items refrigerated or on ice in a cooler at all times.

Sit-Down Meals

Sit-down meals require tables, chairs, adequate space, and more preparation than grab-and-go meals. This type of program is worth considering for some at-risk populations, because sitting down and breaking bread with others can provide important social benefits.

Marginalized adults don't always have a chance to talk to other people. Sitting down at a table together can make otherwise isolated individuals feel like equals. Sit-down meals also provide opportunities for social workers and other community workers to meet and offer these people advice, help, and any services they may need.

At-risk children don't always sit down at the table for regular family meals. Welcoming everyone in the school to a sit-down meal program gives the less fortunate kids a chance to learn proper table manners. Those who are lucky enough to eat family meals together at home will model good table skills for those who don't have that luxury.

Sit-down meals can also be good for kids who have a hard time making friends on the playground. Starting a conversation over a meal at a table is a great way to break the ice and make new friends. And the tables can provide opportunities for homework clubs and for colouring or drawing skills to develop.

A sit-down meal program should teach the kids to clear their tables when they're done. Children who use plates, cups, and cutlery will learn how important it is to clear away their place settings and put their dirty dishes into the proper bins or the dishwasher after eating.

Classroom Meals

Meals served in a classroom can be distracting, depending on how they're set up. But if you make food available right in the classroom, you're more likely to reach all of the children you're targeting.

It's important to encourage every child in the class to enjoy the supplied food. Singling out a few kids can stigmatize them, and they may shy away from your efforts. No one is proud of being poor, and kids will do anything they can to avoid being targeted by their peers. These kids have enough to feel stressed over. Imagine how they'll feel knowing the food is there, but having no access to it because of pride or fear of being treated differently. It's better to include all the kids, even if they don't actually need your help.

Take-Home Meals

Some populations are best served by programs that send people home with pre-made meals or that bring pre-made meals to them.

I worked on a school program in a particularly impoverished area that provided hungry kids with a daily sit-down breakfast and a bagged lunch that they would take to class with them from the program. There was concern that they weren't getting enough to eat on weekends, though, until a local Rotary Club offered to send them home every Friday with backpacks full of nonperishable items to get them through the weekend—boxes of cereal, granola bars, fruit, macaroni and cheese, and so on. The children brought the backpacks back to school each Monday for reuse the following weekend.

You could provide weekly pre-made meals, such as lasagna in disposable containers, for families to take home and cook themselves. These meals could be fresh or frozen. They'd help feed the families for a couple of days.

Or you could provide meals that are already cooked. Meals on Wheels is a well-known example of this type of program for senior citizens who live alone. It can be very difficult to cut and prepare food when your physical abilities start to fail, when your hands become arthritic or you find it painful simply to stand. A supplementary take-home food program is a fantastic way to supply seniors with nutritious meals.

Again, if you supply perishable items, you need to keep them at the proper temperatures during storage and transport.

Catered Meals

A program that offers catered meals on an intermittent basis usually revolves around a holiday such as Christmas, Easter, Valentine's Day, New Year's Day, or Thanksgiving.

In a catered meal program, your volunteers will greet the clients as they arrive, show them to their seats, and serve them beverages followed by plated meals. This is a great program because it's rare for marginalized people to be seated at a table and served by an attendant. It's a special treat for them.

My boys and I used to volunteer for one of these programs. I coached the boys beforehand that the people they'd be serving might be smelly and a little unusual. I made it clear that if they felt uncomfortable at any moment to tell me straight away why, then they could move to the side and just watch, or they could help out behind the scenes. It goes without saying that it is necessary to keep a close watch on any child volunteering around marginalized individuals.

Both boys went up to most of the clients and asked what kind of nonalcoholic beverages they'd like, then served the drinks. The fact that my children weren't freaked out helped put a smile on the clients' faces. It was as if they felt accepted again. Many told the boys they were doing a great job.

Refining Your Goals

Once you've decided on the type of meal program you'll offer, you need to further define your goals. Do you want to offer one meal a month? One a week? One a day, or more than one a day?

As you think this through, be realistic. The program you choose will affect both the budget and the staff resources you'll need.

If you're unsure how many days you want to cook, you can start small and gradually expand from there. If you want to provide a meal every day, for example, start with just two days a week, then add another day each week or each month until you reach your goal. That way, you won't waste food because of low attendance and high expectations. Once you become more popular, you can increase your productivity. It's a lot easier to start small and grow your program than it is to start big and fail!

Think about what you'll serve, and whether you'll make all of the food yourself or have some of it catered in. If your school cafeteria buys its lunches from a catering company, you may be able to buy your breakfasts from the same company. Or you may be able to buy food from another licensed public or private food supplier. Serving meals out of a food truck is another great way to distribute food to people on the street, or even in a school if there's no room for a kitchen.

If you prepare the meals yourself from scratch rather than purchasing pre-made items, you may receive a higher rate of reimbursement from grant funds. This is also cheaper and healthier for your clients than using commercially prepared foods. It will also affect the type of kitchen you'll need.

Chapter 3

Finding the Right Space

Once you've decided on your final goal—the program you're aiming for, not the one you're starting with—you need to find a suitable location. You'll need both a place to prepare the meals and a place where you can distribute them.

What kind of kitchen do you need? How big does it need to be? Does it have to be on site?

What kind of space will you need for serving your clients? How much room will you need? Do you need tables and chairs?

Don't rush! You want to find the *right* place—not just *any* place. It's easy to get carried away with the excitement of starting a program, but keep your goals realistic.

You may be lucky and find a facility where you can both prepare and serve the meals. If the facility doesn't have a kitchen, though, you'll have to build a kitchen there (if you can get permission) or prepare the meals elsewhere and transport them for serving. You might even decide to serve your clients directly out of the truck you use to transport the food to them.

A Place to Serve Your Clients

Suitable spaces are available in a variety of places. You can approach schools, community centres, and churches to see if they have the type of kitchen and the space you need for serving your clients. You might even consider using a private home.

Whatever type of space you choose, plan your details first. Show them to whomever runs the facility, and make sure you have their support before you rent the space. Not only is this respectful, it also makes things run more smoothly. You want this person on your side.

If the manager of the building isn't interested in your program, don't try to go over his or her head. Someone who's forced to take on a program can be most unaccommodating. You don't want this. Look for another facility, or try to work with the manager to come up with a compromise solution.

You will also need to check with local officials and health inspectors to be sure you can host a program in your chosen facility.

Schools

Every school is different, and this will affect the type of program you set up. Each school runs differently, and students' needs can vary widely.

Typically, because high schools are larger than elementary schools, you can expect more meal-program participants in a high school than in an elementary school. Keep this in mind when selecting the room you'll use.

If there's no school cafeteria, make sure the room you choose can accommodate all of the children you expect to use the program. Depending on the type and quality of food you provide, you should expect at least one-third of the school population to participate in a breakfast program, and a little more than one-third to take advantage of a lunch program.

Even if there is a cafeteria, you may not be able to use it. I know of a high school whose kitchen is too small for food prep, so it has its lunches catered in. The contract with the catering company prohibits the school from running a free breakfast program in its own cafeteria. It happens.

It's essential that you find the right room for your program. At-risk children live with uncertainty and change. A safe, consistent, familiar place to go can give them a sense of structure and stability. For ease of access, try to find a room with its own entrance from the outside, especially if your program starts before the school opens.

You can run a meal program out of any useable school room. Just remember that most schools are union environments, so getting maintenance to install a kitchen, a sink, or appliances—basically, anything at all—may take a while.

CLASSROOM

A grab-and-go food program may not be the best choice for a classroom environment, but it allows you to supply food when you can't establish a sit-down program. Grab-and-go items include granola bars, muffins, sandwiches, yogurt, whole fruit—anything children can hold and take with them. Eggs on toast is not an option for a grab-and-go, unless you make it into a sandwich.

If you're going to serve a grab-and-go breakfast in an elementary school, it should be available in each classroom. One way to do this is by having volunteers or the program facilitator drop off the food in containers or bins in the morning, and having children take any remaining food back to the prep room in the afternoon. A child without a lunch can take extra food in the morning and save it for lunchtime, or they can grab something from the bin at noon. There are disadvantages to consider, though, because some parents will take advantage of what they see as a regular lunch option even if they don't need it.

If the food is served in classrooms, it's important that they be open early, or that teachers not worry about kids eating during classes. Yes, eating in class can be distracting, but a fed child learns more and is less disruptive than a hungry one.

In a high school, grab-and-go food should be available in a common area. It's a lot of work—and even redundant—to have grab-and-go options in each classroom in a high school, but it can be done.

Most hungry, malnourished kids have a hard time waking up in the morning, and sometimes arrive at school late. Grab-and-go items should be available for them even if you're providing a sit-down breakfast. And once the at-risk kiddos learn about a breakfast program in their school—whether it's high school or elementary—they start coming to it, and that tardiness problem tends to diminish. Kids discover that they have a good reason to go to school. Hunger will do that to a person.

At first, the children you're most worried about may not come to your program. They may not want the other kids to know their home situations. This is a good reason to open the program to everyone in the school. Eventually, all of the marginalized children will participate, even if they're the last ones to join in.

PLANNING ROOM

The planning room is usually the base classroom for the childcare and youth worker at a school.

Using this room for a meal program is a fantastic idea, because almost all of the at-risk children come here. Since a meal program usually takes just 30 minutes, the childcare and youth worker has the room to themselves for the rest of the day.

And what better way to provide these kids with life skills than by giving the childcare and youth worker access to the kitchen and laundry facilities?

I know of a school that does this, and its childcare and youth worker volunteers with the breakfast program. This shows the kids how much she cares about them. She knows this is a great opportunity to provide life skills the children may be missing, such as how to cook and do laundry. She even works information about expiration dates and recipes into the curriculum for certain children.

INDIGENOUS ROOM

Many schools now have classrooms where the kids learn about local Indigenous cultures, including Indigenous history and traditions, belief systems, stories, songs, and arts and crafts.

An Indigenous classroom is a great place to run a meal program. It gives you a place to feed the kids, and it gives the teacher a chance to interact with the students and perhaps their family members. It's great exposure for both the teacher and the kids, whether they're Indigenous or not.

Playing traditional music in the classroom, having Indigenous pictures to colour on the tables, playing the drum—anything is possible if the right teacher is given the opportunity and goes with it.

GYMNASIUM

Many school gymnasiums have attached cafeterias with kitchen facilities. The school gym can therefore be a good place for a hot-meal program.

The main issue you'll face is availability. A morning practice can screw up a good breakfast if a basketball lands in your plate. And tables and chairs have to be put away before the gym can be used. This may be a problem if you're behind on your clean-up.

One solution is to use a separate room for serving and eating, and to use the gym's kitchen just for cooking and washing up.

Remember, if you can't serve it immediately, you must keep hot food in chafing dishes or a steam table and cold food on ice, to prevent bacterial growth.

Community Centres

Many community centres have kitchens, whether large or small. I once saw a fantastic commercial kitchen in an ice rink facility, with a couple of rooms available to rent for functions.

Even if they have commercial kitchens, not every community centre wants to run meal programs of their own. They may be interested in collaborating with you, though. Approach your local facilities, especially if they're run by nonprofit organizations, and ask whether they can provide space for your program.

I know of a Boys and Girls Club in a very high-risk area that's used for food programs for the elementary school next door. An organization called the Soroptimists used to fund and run a breakfast program here, and the Boys and Girls Club itself runs an after-school snack program out of the same room.

Churches

Churches are usually interested in helping the less fortunate and may be willing to provide space—and volunteers—for meal programs. Many have nice kitchen facilities.

If your church has no kitchen, you'll need to install some basic appliances or have the meals catered in. In the long run, installing a small kitchen can be cheaper than catering—and it will be beneficial for other church functions. To get started, you'll need a properly working refrigerator, a deep freezer, a stove, a couple of sinks, and a commercial dishwasher. These items can be found inexpensively, especially if you watch Internet buy-and-sell sites such as Craigslist.

If you find a church with a small kitchen that nevertheless wants to go really big with a food program—and has the money—consider installing a commercial kitchen before you launch your program.

One church I know of started with a small kitchen, then expanded its program as time went by, and eventually installed an incredible $300,000 kitchen. That's a lot of money! They went all out, putting in a walk-in cooler and all the bells and whistles. Now they can hold multiple functions, and even rent out the kitchen and facility to generate income for both the meal program and the church.

Before you start building any kind of kitchen, find out whether the city requires a permit and/or inspections during and after construction. You don't want any unpleasant surprises later!

Private Homes

It's rare, but some people like to feed others so much that they open up their homes to the needy.

If you're one of these people, we all commend you. Please be aware, though, that there are risks you may not have considered.

You'll need liability insurance in case someone is hurt on your property. You may also need a license to run food out of your home kitchen. You can find out about this by calling city hall.

And of course you run the risk of theft when you invite marginalized people into your home. When they see where you live, you may become a target—whether you believe this could happen or not. Some of these people are in dire straits, and will do almost anything to escape their situations. Sadly, some people have been tossed aside throughout their lives and have difficulty making emotional human connections. No connection means no respect, no protectiveness, no regret. So even though you're helping them, if they're desperate enough and see what you have in your home, they may come back and steal it. It isn't personal—for them, it's survival.

A Suitable Kitchen

Once you find a facility to host your program, you need to look at your kitchen set-up. Planning ahead is imperative. Why build a two-lane highway if you'll need four lanes in the future?

Too many times I've walked into gorgeous fine-dining restaurants only to see that their kitchens are no bigger than my bathroom. That means two people have to squeeze themselves in and cook for a 60-seat restaurant. Whoever designed these places wasn't thinking of their future potential.

If you think you'll want to expand your kitchen in the future, keep this in mind when setting up your starter kitchen. Pay a professional to draft a blueprint of what you'll eventually want, and craft your starter kitchen around that.

Figuring out what kind of kitchen you need can be tricky. I recommend that you consult a few people who know kitchens.

First, ask a chef or kitchen manager for advice. Get at least two opinions. People love to feel that their advice is well regarded, so don't be afraid to ask the head chefs at your local restaurants for their advice. You'll not only make them feel important, you'll also make connections in your community. You may even find that they're willing to help with menu planning.

Once you have expert advice from a couple of professionals, I recommend that you hire a professional designer to create your kitchen layout. If you're on a tight budget, you might ask a university or college interior design or drafting student to do this work. The teacher may even grade the student on your project, making it free (or nearly free) for you as well as a portfolio item for the student. If you are planning a kitchen in a school, the maintenance crew will work with you to build the space.

If you're lucky enough to find a space that already has a nice kitchen, you'll need to determine its suitability for the type of service you intend to provide, and make any necessary adjustments.

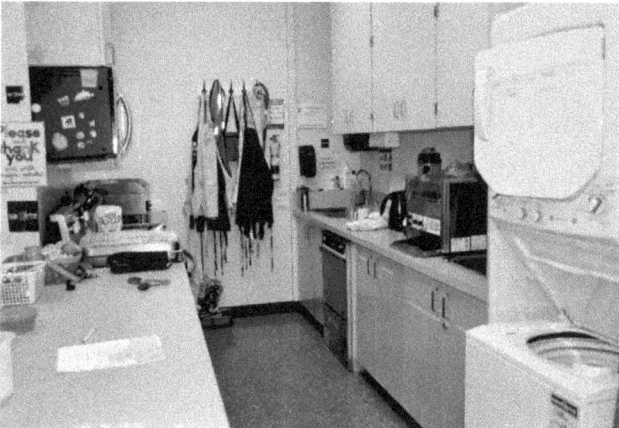

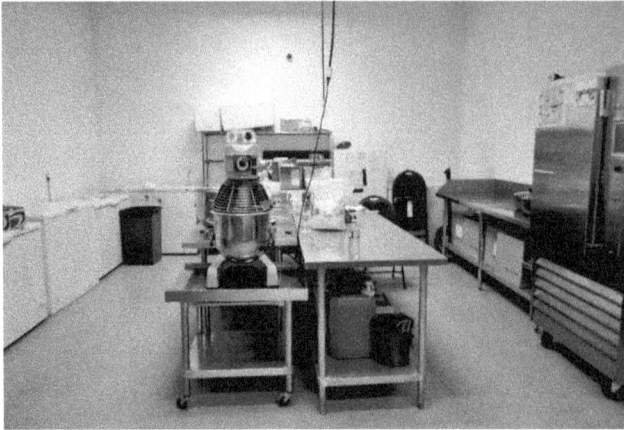

Outfitting Your Kitchen

While a commercial kitchen is the ideal (and may also bring in revenue, if you're able to rent it to the public), it's not necessary. A basic kitchen may suit you nicely, as long as it's properly outfitted.

When choosing equipment, think about what you really need—not just what you'd like to have. A small program can operate with a regular stove and oven. If you plan to rent out the kitchen, though, a convection oven might be a good purchase.

The following are essential items for most food program kitchens:

o   Counter and storage space
o   Double sink
o   Stove with oven
o   Microwave
o   Refrigerator
o   Free-standing freezer (i.e., separate from the refrigerator)
o   Dishwasher with sanitation cycle
o   Apple slicer
o   Commercial toaster
o   Blender
o   Chef's knives in different sizes
o   Knife sharpener
o   Mixing bowls
o   Ladle
o   Slotted spoons
o   Large spoons
o   Large and small whisks
o   Kitchen tongs
o   Vegetable peeler
o   Rubber spatula
o   Food turner (also called a metal spatula or a pancake flipper)
o   Kitchen scissors
o   Wooden spoons
o   Basting brush
o   Potato masher
o   Can opener
o   Grater
o   Forks, knives, and spoons
o   Glasses, mugs, plates, and bowls
o   Pots and pans with lids
o   Large cooking pot

- ○   Nonstick frying pans
- ○   Hot plate (also called a griddle)
- ○   Parchment paper
- ○   Saran wrap
- ○   Large and small refrigerator/freezer bags
- ○   Strainer
- ○   Cutting boards
- ○   Measuring cups
- ○   Measuring spoons
- ○   Rolling pin
- ○   Baking sheets
- ○   Muffin tins
- ○   Hotel pans (the square or rectangular pans you often see in buffet steam tables and cooling areas—the food is both cooked and served in these pans)
- ○   Range hood
- ○   Dishcloths, towels, and rags
- ○   Oven mitts
- ○   Hot pads
- ○   Aprons
- ○   Chefs' uniforms or cooks' clothes
- ○   Cooks' hats or hairnets
- ○   Bag clips
- ○   Refrigerator thermometer
- ○   Freezer thermometer
- ○   Steam table, or chafing dishes and fuel if there's no steam table
- ○   Meat thermometer
- ○   Oven thermometer
- ○   Sign-in binder
- ○   Recipe binder
- ○   Broom
- ○   Dustpan
- ○   Pitchers

The following items aren't typically essential, but they're nice to have:

o   Two sinks that are well separated from one another
       Use one sink for washing hands and dishes, and use the other sink for washing fruits and vegetables. This may be mandatory in some areas.
o   A tap with a high arch, preferably with a pull-out spray hose
o   A commercial dishwasher
       A regular dishwasher has a sanitation cycle of more than an hour, whereas a commercial dishwasher has a sanitation cycle of a couple of minutes. When you clean up after your shift and turn on the dishwasher, who's going to unload and reload it with the rest of the dirty dishes? A commercial dishwasher is well worth the money.
o   Stainless steel countertops
       They're not only the best choice for hygiene, they're also the best option if you have a commercial dishwasher set under the counter, because they won't warp when exposed to the heat of the dishwasher's sanitation cycle.
o   A washer and dryer
       You'll need to wash dishcloths, towels, rags, and aprons, so an in-house washer and dryer can be a godsend. An upright set-up saves space. You can also use these appliances to wash your clients' clothes, if you decide to provide that service. A school I know of washes the dirty jackets, coats, and clothes of at-risk kids, dressing them in cleaned lost-and-found clothes while their own clothes are in the washer and dryer. The kids wear the lost-and-found garments home, carrying their clean clothes, and bring the borrowed garments back the next day.
o   A three-slice commercial rotating toaster
       If you're serving breakfast to a large group, a three-slicer is better than a two-slice commercial rotating toaster. It will increase your production of toasted items and get the job done faster. It's totally worth the money!

o   Some type of stand-alone mixer

This item makes your life a lot easier, especially if you're making a lot of items from scratch.

o   An oven that heats up quickly

This is important if you have only a short time for cooking. A convection oven is best, but it's expensive, so look for an oven that heats up in five minutes or less. I once worked with an oven that took 15 minutes to heat up, and it made my life difficult.

o   Good knives

A knife that can keep a sharp edge is among a chef's most important tools. A knife that won't hold its edge is dangerous. Ever try cutting a tomato with a dull knife? Safety matters, and a knife that can slip and cut someone is not safe.

o   A commercial blender

This is fabulous if you have items like smoothies on the menu.

o   Commercial food processor such as a Robot Coupe

This brand does everything. It's the best kind to use for mass production.

o   Commercial mixer such as a KitchenAid heavy-duty mixer

This brand is a great choice for medium-scale food production.

The type of program you're planning will determine how many bowls, utensils, and other kitchen items you'll need. If you're unsure, more is always better than less.

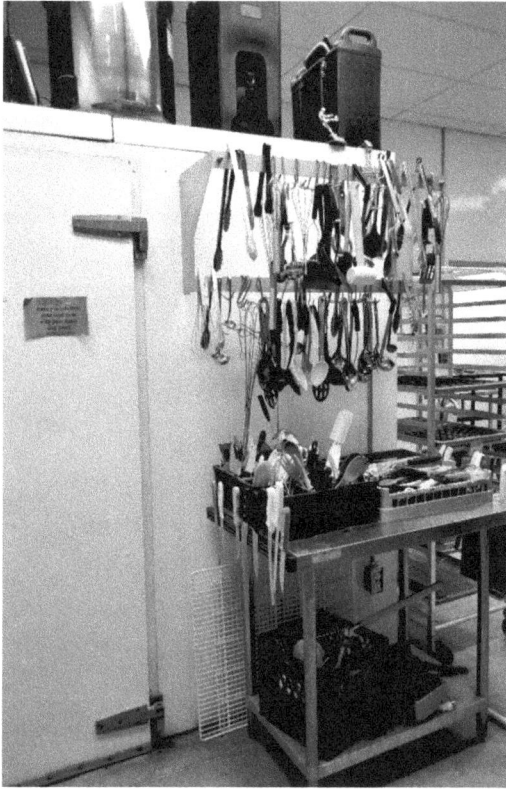

Chapter 4

Finding the Right Staff

Once you've decided on a program type and found a suitable space with the right kitchen facilities, you need to determine who will do the work. Running a food program takes person-power.

You'll need people to do the following:

- Coordinate the program
- Order the food
- Prepare the meals
- Deliver and/or serve the meals
- Clean up the kitchen
- Do the paperwork
- Raise the funds

You can assign one person to do several (or even all) of these jobs, or you can find one person for each job. It all depends on the type of staff you have and the size of your program.

I know of care facilities where one chef and one prep person/dishwasher prepare and plate meals for more than 150 residents. You can get by with only two people in the kitchen if everything is well prepared and executed. Prepping the food for the next day, for example, ensures that it will be ready to go with minimal stress. I've even worked alone at a care facility, cooking and serving three full meals a day for forty-five residents, then washing the dishes and cleaning up.

Working a kitchen this way typically requires a skilled experienced cook. An experienced cook usually costs more than someone with less training and experience.

Will you use volunteers, paid staff, or a combination? Do your staff need to be certified? Do you need liability insurance? We'll examine each of these questions later in this chapter.

Specific Roles

Program Coordinator

Finding a coordinator for your food program can be challenging. You need someone with fire in their belly, because every successful program is driven by someone with passion. This person will probably be you, at least to begin with.

The program coordinator is the head of the entire operation. They recruit and manages staff, sets and implements the budget, communicates with the facility managers, ensures that reports are filed, and makes sure the program has enough money. They therefore work closely with the head cook, the paperwork coordinator, and the fundraising coordinator.

The program coordinator needs to be on site every day at first. They must be able to cover any open shifts, no matter what the role, either by recruiting and training volunteers or by taking the shifts themselves.

The person you choose must be able to coordinate multiple activities, communicate effectively, resolve conflicts, find solutions when there are problems, and manage people. They need good organizational and interpersonal skills. Kitchen experience is an asset.

Whether you make the program coordinator a paid position or a volunteer role, it's a *job*. It must be taken seriously. The entire operation turns on the coordinator's ability to keep things running smoothly.

Head Cook

Front-loading is critical to a successful program. If you can, choose someone with industry experience to lead your kitchen.

An experienced cook or chef can control food costs and stretch the budget. This person knows when and how to place mass orders, saving money for the program. They also know how to coordinate staff and prepare meals for many people at once.

Your head chef should be someone who has cooked in a restaurant, a seniors' home, or some other food-service facility—not just at home. Choose someone with solid industry experience, and they can train everyone else in your program.

A head cook needs a solid grasp of food preparation techniques, safe cooking temperatures, food-storage standards, and food-safety regulations. They must be able to work quickly while keeping the kitchen clean and organized. It's essential that this person hold high-level certification in food safety.

It's the head cook's responsibility to monitor and ensure that exact measurements are used in all food items, while ensuring food quality and determining portion sizes. They should be able to lift up to twenty-five kilograms (fifty-five pounds). It's helpful if they also have first-aid training.

Like the program coordinator's role, the head cook's job is critical to your program's success. It's a key position that requires commitment, whether the person volunteers or is paid.

Cook's Helpers, Servers, Cleaners, and Other Staff

In addition to the chef, a prep person is a huge asset. This person can be a volunteer or a paid staffer. A professional cook will be able to show the prep person what to do.

The prep person, like the chef, must have a certificate in food safety. They are responsible for cutting, portioning, following recipes, baking, labelling and putting orders away, helping with clean-up, and writing prep lists. The ideal candidate has good organizational skills and can lift up to twenty-five kilograms (fifty-five pounds). First-aid training is an asset.

In most programs where people line up to get their food, the kitchen staff also function as servers. It doesn't take long to serve meals over a counter. For sit-down meals, though, you may need extra people to bring plates to and from the tables and clean up the eating area after the meal.

Some facilities like to provide table service just for special occasions. I know of one that does this for their homeless clientele at Thanksgiving and Christmas. They go the full nine yards, with tablecloths, decorations, and fancy glasses and dishes. These people rarely experience this kind of service in their daily lives, so it's a special treat for them.

The number of people you need depends on the number of clients you have and the complexity of your menu.

If you're running a breakfast program for ninety elementary school kids, you'll need an experienced chef or two well-trained helpers in the kitchen.

If you're running a supper program for ninety adults, however, you'll need a professional chef or experienced cook and two helpers, or three or four well-trained volunteers. An experienced chef should be able to prepare a meal for forty-five people by themselves, but will need help for more than forty-five clients.

If you decide to offer sit-down meals, either occasionally or on a regular basis, you'll need to schedule two or three servers for every forty clients, plus an experienced cook with an experienced helper to dish out the food in the back and a coordinator to make sure the program is running on point.

It's essential that everyone on your team uses good prep lists, to-do lists, and clean-up lists.

Paperwork Coordinator

You'll need an organized person to do the paperwork. This includes saving receipts, filling out forms, preparing reports at the end of each month and year, and writing grant applications. Most grants require you to file a report every month, and provide a form for this. Many ask you to indicate client numbers, volunteer numbers, food costs, and other expenses.

You can do this job yourself, work with a friend, or delegate the task to someone else. Choose someone you trust who is good with computers. In one school, I provided the principal with all of the information, and she filled out the necessary forms on her computer. Keeping records doesn't take long if everything is tallied up as you bring in your receipts.

Keep *all* receipts and any other information you'll need for the monthly and yearly reports. Place them in an envelope in a safe place, or in a zipped plastic folder that stays in the sign-in binder, so everything is together.

Make copies of everything for your own records, and put them in a binder or folder, so you'll have something to refer to if you have to send the originals elsewhere. Paper trails are good!

It's useful to keep all of your personnel information in a binder, too. This includes staff schedules, sign-in sheets, signed confidentiality agreements, and volunteers' phone numbers and email addresses. When it's time to file reports, you'll have everything you need in one place.

Be sure to keep a temperature record sheet for every appliance that has a cold or hot setting. Assign someone to read the thermometers inside the refrigerator and freezer at a specific time each day, and record the temperatures. This ensures that each appliance runs at the optimal food-safe temperature, and alerts you if there's a change. Never rely on an appliance's built-in temperature recorder. Instead, purchase a new Celsius thermometer that goes down to twenty degrees below zero.

Fundraising Coordinator

Nothing happens without money.

As we'll see in Chapter 8, funding for a food program is often available from a variety of sources. You may be lucky enough to secure stable funding from a single source, or you may have to use several strategies to raise the funds your program needs.

Whatever your situation, you'll need a dedicated person to oversee and coordinate your fundraising activities. This is a long-term role. Look for someone who is experienced with marketing, sales, community outreach, and/or fundraising within the nonprofit sector. Make sure this person is upbeat and personable and believes in your cause.

Skill Requirements

Running a meal program takes commitment and skill. It's best if you or your staff have some experience in the food industry.

It's also important that someone on staff have good interpersonal skills and/or experience in dealing with vulnerable people. At-risk children and adults are often sensitive to things that we might not expect to upset them. Your clients need to be comfortable in the environment you create, or they won't come back.

When I started my first school breakfast program, I had a significant culinary background and knew how to run a kitchen, but I was inexperienced both in running a charitable food program and in dealing with vulnerable people. Over time, I found it beneficial to have staff members who could deal with sensitive people who were at risk for abuse, delinquency, and worse.

Ask prospective staff members whether they have training or experience in dealing with troubled individuals. Ask about their interactions with at-risk populations, and listen carefully to their answers. Try to determine how they'll react if a situation becomes volatile.

Safety comes first. Before they start working for you, give your staff members the skills they'll need to deal with vulnerable individuals who may say or do unpredictable things. Your workers may have to deal with vulgar language, poor hygiene, drug or alcohol use, conflict, and more. Be sure they have the appropriate skills for dealing with these situations, and that they're prepared, comfortable, and nonjudgmental when the unexpected does happen. Look for community and night-school programs to help provide this training.

Volunteers or Employees?

If your funding is already secured, you can determine exactly how much you can spend, and therefore whether you can afford to hire someone. You can run your program with paid staff, volunteers, or both.

Volunteers are the best way to keep program costs low. Volunteers are wonderful! They usually love to help out, which is great for morale.

Unfortunately, some people don't think showing up and showing commitment to a volunteer job is as important as you think it is. You must make it absolutely clear that volunteering involves commitment, just as a paid job does. It's everyone's responsibility to show up on time and do the work they're trained for.

Paid employees are more likely to show up, and they will probably take the job more seriously. You might want to put paid employees in key roles and use volunteers for other tasks.

Even if you start solely with volunteers, you'll need more people as your program grows, and eventually you'll probably need paid employees. When you have paid, experienced staff, you can operate with fewer people. If you're planning to feed many clients over the long term, it's good to start with at least one paid employee who has at least a few years of professional kitchen experience.

Use your paid employee(s) to train and oversee your volunteers. Sometimes volunteers will take direction better from someone who is in charge if they are in a paid position rather than in a volunteer position. In my experience, paying someone gives them authority.

Running a program strictly with volunteers can be risky. Even if someone signs a contract or makes a commitment to volunteer for a certain length of time, they can pull out whenever they like. People often leave volunteer positions when something else comes up.

If yours is primarily a volunteer-based program, you'll need at least two volunteers per shift, and each volunteer should work just one shift per week. Schedule them for more than that, and they can burn out. I've seen it happen many times.

If you're hiring paid staff, you can probably get by with one full-time employee for up to forty-five clients. If you have more clients, you'll need more staff. You'll need to increase your staff as your program grows.

Finding Volunteers

Newspaper and online advertising are effective ways to find volunteers. Word of mouth is also helpful.

Keep your eyes open for people who always seem to want to help. You want people who can give and follow directions. They should also be organized, energetic, interested, and good with kids or at-risk populations.

Choose people who aren't already overwhelmed with other things. When you approach a candidate, look for signs of excitement. If the person says, "Oh, ummm, well, let me think about it," offer to call back in a couple of days. You never know what's going on in people's lives. Don't be discouraged if you don't hear "I'd love to!" right off the bat. Sometimes it takes a few days for the idea to sink in.

On the other hand, if there's still no excitement in the person's voice when you make your next contact, move on. Vulnerable people need to be greeted with a smile, not faced with someone who simply couldn't say no to you.

Schools

Most schools have Parent Advisory Committees, or PACs (also known as Parent Teacher Associations, or PTAs). Sometimes the PAC helps fund and staff the food program.

Be careful not to rely too heavily on a PAC, though. There are strong PACs and not-so-strong PACs, and they can vary from year to year. Some have members who don't get along or who have difficulty working together. A broken PAC could mean the end of your program, especially if they can't find a parent to take it on.

Sometimes a PAC wishes to contribute money, but no work. In this case, ask them to pay for the program coordinator, the head cook, or the food. This reduces the amount of money you have to raise by other means.

Parents, teachers, and students can volunteer to help with meal programs. Put out an open request for parents and other relatives to volunteer for your program. You may hear from parents who want to volunteer with the school but don't want to be part of the PAC. Student volunteers can be helpful, too, as long as volunteering doesn't expose them to confidential information that could stigmatize the children your program serves.

Volunteering in a school program is a year-long commitment, so safeguard your human resources. I recommend that each volunteer take only one shift per week. Some people may ask for more shifts at first, and you may think this is great, but, trust me, it isn't. Very few people can do more than one shift a week for the entire school year. In my experience, most will burn out and quit the program, leaving you with multiple shifts to fill. If you assign just one shift per person per week, you'll have happier volunteers and a more stable program.

Sometimes schools will have students volunteer with the program. It's great for their resumes and it provides life skills. Confidentiality is key, though, so stress the need to keep any sensitive information they may overhear to themselves. This can be hard for some children who like to gossip.

Religious Organizations

A church, mosque, temple, or synagogue is a wonderful place to recruit volunteers. After all, most religious organizations are founded on a commitment to serve others, especially people in need.

Religious organizations attract people from all walks of life and with all sorts of experience, so you'll undoubtedly find some with culinary experience. A congregation may be big enough to fill all of your volunteer slots.

A religious congregation could even help you raise money for your program, either by helping out temporarily until you find a secure source of funding or by sponsoring your program itself.

A note of caution, though: if members of a congregation volunteer in a food program outside of their faith, they must understand that they are not to preach religion to anyone using the program. This is especially important if the program is based in a school.

Restaurants

Restaurants, especially chains, love to give back to their communities. They're a great source of volunteers for your meal program.

Not all restaurant managers want their staff to volunteer on a regular basis, though. Restaurants are usually busy at night, and employees who work at night and then volunteer regularly during the day can burn out. You may find it most rewarding to ask them to volunteer only occasionally, for special events.

Restaurant employees are wonderful resources. They can help train other volunteers and may be able to help you create a nutritious, appealing menu.

They may also be able to use their own relationships with food distributers to lower your food costs. The minimum order for most Canadian food distributors is usually around $500. For a small food program, that's next to impossible to come up with each week, or even each month. Restaurants order in large quantities, though, and can simply add what you need to their own orders. You get the benefit of bulk pricing without having to order in bulk yourself.

Keep the proper food temperatures in mind when you pick up and transfer food provided by restaurants.

Grocery Stores

A good connection with a grocery store is a wonderful resource. Most grocery stores place a high value on community involvement and are therefore generous. They can provide both volunteers and products for your program.

Some grocery stores like to help for specified periods of time, or even for one day a week.

Superstore volunteered for one breakfast program I ran, and they asked what we needed beforehand. We gave them a list of items we needed. At the end of their volunteering shift, they presented us with a KitchenAid mixer. I was so overwhelmed by their generosity that I cried. They also gave us twelve $100 gift cards so we could purchase more groceries for our program.

PriceSmart helped by delivering food items directly to us in refrigerated trucks. We didn't have to worry about inconsistent temperatures while transporting perishables.

When Costco came to volunteer, they gave us many of the smaller items on our list. Then one of their employees came back and gave us a rolling pin, after she'd had to use a food-oil spray can to roll out the dough while helping us make cinnamon buns. It was wonderful to get a real rolling pin!

A grocery store can help your program in many ways. All you have to do is call or visit the store and ask to speak with the manager. Explain your situation and ask whether the store would like to become a part of the program, either by providing volunteers, donating food, delivering food, or whatever else might help you. You're unlikely to walk away with nothing.

Seniors' Organizations

Retired people often have time on their hands. Not only are seniors typically well seasoned in the kitchen, but many are looking for something meaningful to be a part of. Helping with a food program can give them purpose.

So, where do you find seniors? Start with a seniors' centre. Connect with religious groups and service clubs such as Rotary International or Soroptimists International. Put up notices in recreation centres and libraries, where seniors like to gather.

Seniors make some of the best volunteers because they usually take their volunteering responsibilities seriously. Many older people travel, though, and some have health complications that may restrict their involvement in your program. Plan accordingly.

Banks

Banking is another industry that loves community involvement. Talk to the manager of your local bank about sponsoring your program, either by providing volunteers or by helping you raise money.

Bank employees understand both customer service and financial principles—and they have contacts in the local business community. If your local bank can't provide volunteers to help you prepare and serve meals, it may be able to provide publicity and expertise for a fundraising campaign.

Firefighters

Firefighters are involved in food programs throughout the community where I live. They sponsor programs and volunteer their time. It's fabulous.

Call or visit your local firehall and ask to talk to the chief. Ask whether his or her firefighters would like to volunteer in your program. Firefighters as enthusiastic cooks may be a cliché, but it's for good reason.

Local Businesses

Most local businesses want to be seen as good neighbours who give back to the community. They know their clients are local, and they want to reach as many as they can.

Participating in a food program is an excellent way for a business to develop relationships with community members. This exposure is a most effective form of advertising and will make the businesses look good within the community.

Community Service Groups

Organizations that are dedicated to community service can be a great source of volunteers. Consider approaching your local Rotary, Soroptimist, and veterans' clubs to ask for help.

These organizations can provide both volunteers and connections to local businesses. Many groups also raise funds for special projects.

Hiring Paid Staff

Running a food program is eighty percent about food and twenty percent about ordering, paperwork, scheduling, and funding. Someone with a culinary background has experience in these areas and can alleviate many of your worries.

Paid employees with culinary experience are better equipped to deal with hiccups, improvising or changing meal items on the fly. If you run out of muffin mix because someone forgot to order it or the store was out of the product, for example, experienced staff can change the menu quickly.

You can find paid staff through newspaper and online advertising, as well as by word of mouth. Talk to any contacts you have in the restaurant industry—they always know people who are looking for work.

Orientation and Training

Once you have all your people in place, hold a group meeting and introduce them to one another. Some may volunteer only one day a week and so will never meet otherwise.

Go over the purpose of the program, explaining how it will work and how each person will contribute to its success. Emphasize the vulnerable nature of your clients, and explain how best to deal with them. Provide guidelines for maintaining confidentiality, respect, and discretion. Answer any questions or concerns as they arise.

Ask everyone to sign an agreement. The volunteers should sign a volunteer and confidentiality agreement, and the paid chef should sign an employment agreement. If you're running a school program, the school may be able to provide agreements for your people to sign. It is important to keep all signed agreements in a safe place where only you or a few privileged staff have access to it.

Acquaint everyone with the personnel binder, staff contact information, schedules, and sign-in sheets. Make sure they all know where it is and how to use it. Make sure they know who to contact and what to do in an emergency. Someone with first-aid training should always be on site, so be sure everyone knows who that is. Ensure that everyone knows how to fill out an accident report.

After the meeting, you and your head cook can train each person in more depth on the job. Teach them what they need to know as they work. I've had volunteers who didn't know how to hold a knife properly. I showed them on the job, and they learned fast.

Some people may try to sign up for multiple volunteer shifts right at the beginning. Don't let them. It's incredible how fast people can burn out, and it's the last thing you need. Set a reasonable schedule that doesn't overtax your human resources.

As a chef in a retirement home, I have prepared meals for more than 120 people in one sitting, all by myself. A trained chef will find it easy to cook for 40 to 100 people. But the average volunteer can find it overwhelming and not know where to begin. Be patient. Some of your volunteers won't be experienced. Some may be volunteering just to learn how to cook! It doesn't matter why they're there—they've shown up, and you need them. A few shifts, and most will catch on quickly. If you train your staff well, your program will succeed.

You must teach proper handwashing and food-handling techniques right at the start. You may feel embarrassed about correcting people, and worried about upsetting them, but you must assume that they don't know anything and it's your job to teach them. You're in charge. They'll listen to you.

Be kind about everything, but be firm, and correct them if they forget.

"Hey, Jennifer, please remember to wash your hands before handling the food. Thanks!" Say it with a smile.

"Gavin, I don't know if you know this, because each place is different, but here we don't use the same cutting board twice. The other cutting boards are in that cupboard. You can use any one of those. Please and thanks!" Smile!

Running a meal program can be stressful, especially when you're starting out, but please remember that your disposition is critical. There's nothing keeping your volunteers here except their big hearts. Go easy on them, especially if they have limited kitchen experience. Volunteers will give a lot of free hours—possibly thousands. It's important that they know they're appreciated.

This is equally true for paid employees. Morale is critical to any food program, and you want everyone to come to work smiling. Sometimes theirs are the only smiles your clients see all day. Appreciation is key!

Remind all your people that they hold lives in their hands. This means they have to wash their hands *all the time*. After they touch raw meat. After they mix dough with their hands. Even when they think their hands aren't dirty.

This is critically important, especially if any of your clients have allergies. If you were to touch some peanuts, not wash your hands because your hands "weren't dirty," then pick up a piece of toast and butter and serve it to someone you had no idea was severely allergic to nuts, the consequences could be deadly.

Make sure your staff take handwashing seriously. I can't stress this enough.

Certifications

To get a municipal permit to run a kitchen, you'll probably have to show that your staff members are certified in food safety. Some kind of certification in food hygiene or food handling is usually mandatory. Your kitchen must also pass a health inspection.

Each city has its own way of doing things, so check to see what yours requires. You don't want to be shut down before you start!

Foodsafe

In British Columbia, where I lived and worked, Foodsafe certification is required to work with food that's served to the public. Foodsafe is British Columbia's food-safety training program. On each shift, you must have at least one front-line food-service worker (e.g., a cook, server, busperson, or dishwasher) who holds the Foodsafe Level 1 certification. This provides training in cooking temperatures, cooling temperatures, food-handling techniques, hygiene, and the dangers of cross-contamination.

Food can kill if it's not handled correctly. People who live on the street often have weakened immune systems, both because of health complications and because of their living conditions. Not everyone lives on the street, of course. Some of your clients may be senior citizens. Or they may come from families who are struggling financially, particularly if their children require frequent visits to doctors and hospitals. It costs money to buy gas, parking, medication, and products that can boost quality of life. These children may also have weakened immune systems. If they consume food that's been improperly stored and therefore contains bacteria, it could make them seriously ill—or worse.

A Foodsafe Level 2 certification is available, but it's typically not mandatory for a meal program. It's designed for people who manage and supervise teams of food handlers.

Display your Foodsafe (or equivalent) certificate on the wall of your facility, together with your health department's license to cook for the public.

HACCP

Hazard Analysis and Critical Control Points (HACCP) is a system for preventing biological, chemical, and physical hazards that can make food unsafe. Various organizations provide HACCP training and certification.

In a HACCP training program, you'll learn about bacteria, viruses, and parasites, proper cleaning techniques, risk prevention, and correct preparation techniques, including packaging and distributing. HACCP goes into more depth than Foodsafe does.

It's a good idea to have at least one person with an HACCP certification on your team, even if they aren't always on site. This person can teach the rest of your staff about proper food handling, chemical labelling, and product use. This keeps your program on the up-and-up, especially if you're providing bagged lunches or take-home meals.

Legal Issues

Every food program is subject to various rules and regulations. You'll need to deal with most or all of the following, depending on whether your staff are volunteers or employees:

- Permits
- Occupational safety and health

- Labour laws
- Criminal-record checks
- Employment or volunteer agreements
- Confidentiality agreements
- Taxes and workers' compensation
- Insurance

Permits

You'll need a permit from the city's health department before you can launch your meal program.

Every jurisdiction has different regulations for business licenses and health permits, so check with city hall and your local health authority for information.

Occupational Safety and Health

Every food-service facility must conform to regional and national regulations about occupational safety and health. You need to know the regulations and guidelines for working with hazardous products.

In Canada, we have the Workplace Hazardous Materials Information System (WHMIS). The United States has the Hazard Communication Standard (HCS). Both are closely aligned with the Globally Harmonized System of Classification and Labelling of Chemicals (GHS), which was developed by the United Nations. The goal of GHS is to have all countries use the same set of rules for classifying hazards and the same format and content for product labels and safety data sheets.

These systems define and classify chemical hazards and specify how safety information is to be communicated to workers. They specify how containers are to be labelled, and they issue material safety data sheets (MSDS) that tell workers how to protect themselves when working with or near hazardous materials. Most governments can point you toward training for your workers.

This is more important than you might think. You'll be dealing with chemicals such as commercial dishwasher detergent and cleaning solutions, and you need to know what the little pictures and warning signs on the containers mean. You need to know what to do if someone touches or ingests a hazardous product. And if you pour any of these chemicals into unmarked bottles, you need to correctly label the bottles.

Labour Laws

Paying an outsider to run a food program in a school or a community centre could conflict with union rules and labour laws. Find out what the rules are. You may not be allowed to use volunteers.

If hiring someone from the outside takes this job away from a teacher, a teaching assistant, or a school district employee, you might need to find an insider for the position. This may be more expensive; however, an upside of using an insider is that the person will already know the students and have a rapport with parents and teachers.

An insider may also have access to private information about the students, and therefore be able to ensure that at-risk kids get what they need. They are likely to know what allergies the kids have, so you can offer them alternatives without the risk of cross-contamination.

You may be able to bypass a school's union issues by contracting with a catering company. This is considerably more expensive than hiring individual workers, but in the long run, it's more reliable. The caterers will always show up, and one experienced person may be able to handle the entire job. This means you won't have to rely on volunteers to keep your program running. Your budget will determine whether you can hire a catering company.

Some community centres are run by nonprofit organizations, such as Big Brothers. If you want to run a program in a community centre, you must follow its rules and ensure that your program doesn't conflict with any of its other programs.

Criminal-Record Checks

In most schools, it's mandatory that any adult working in close proximity to children undergo a criminal-record check. This is especially important for a food program, because the children you serve are already vulnerable. They shouldn't be exposed to anyone who may have a history as a predator or a criminal.

This is also true for both children and at-risk adults participating in meal programs in other places, such as churches and community centres.

It's therefore very important that you do a criminal-record check on every volunteer and employee, especially if your program involves minors. Have each prospective volunteer or employee go to the local police station and fill out a criminal-record-check form. The police will then let you know whether that person has a criminal record.

Employment or Volunteer Agreements

You should ask each of your employees—whether they're paid staff members or volunteers—to sign a contract letter outlining the terms of their agreement with you, including their duties, obligations, and, if appropriate, remuneration details.

The contract letter should include all of the following:

- The meal program's name and address
- The employee's name, address, telephone number, emergency contact information, and email address
- Whether the employee is a paid staff member or a volunteer
- The employee's title
- The employee's start date
- Whether the position is permanent or temporary (and, if the latter, the anticipated end date)
- The employee's expected hours of work

- The employee's duties and responsibilities
- A confidentiality clause
- The expected dress code
- What the program will supply for the employee's use
- What the employee is expected to supply for his or her own use
- The employee's remuneration, if any
- The employee's vacation entitlement, if any
- Space for the signatures of the employee and the program coordinator
- The date the employee and the program coordinator signed the contract

This information can be in point form or paragraph form. The important thing is to be able to easily find and read all of the details.

After you and the employee have both signed the agreement, place a copy in your personnel file and give the employee a copy.

Confidentiality Agreements

Every member of your staff, paid or volunteer, should also sign a confidentially agreement. They may be exposed to sensitive information about your clients. Keep the signed confidentiality agreements in your personnel binder.

Taxes and Workers' Compensation

When you have paid staff, you need to submit money and reports to the government on their behalf. These include provincial or state and federal income tax, pension-plan contributions, and workers' compensation.

A bookkeeper will know how to deal with this. You'll need to hire a professional or find a qualified volunteer.

Insurance

You also need liability insurance. If the facility doesn't carry insurance, you need to arrange for it before you do anything else. People fall, food becomes contaminated, accidents happen. You know this—so cover yourself!

Call an insurance provider and ask what type of insurance you need. Explain what your program does, what type of facility and workspace you have, what kind of food you serve, and whether your staff are volunteers or paid employees.

It may be possible to add your program to the building's insurance policy as part of your rental agreement. If not, you'll have to obtain and pay for coverage yourself.

Chapter 5

Setting Menus

The meal you serve may be the only food your clients will have all day. Make it as nutritious as possible.

You may want to start off with food items that are more familiar to your clientele until they start coming on a regular basis, then gradually introduce healthier options. Many vulnerable individuals have never eaten a lot of nutritious foods, and may be overwhelmed or turned off if that's all you give them. The axiom that people will eat anything if they're hungry enough isn't always true. I find that gradually introducing more healthful choices works especially well in a school environment.

Always try to offer a fruit or vegetable option with your meal. If you serve juice, dilute it so it's fifty percent water to reduce the sugar content. People won't mind if it tastes diluted. The best option is freshly squeezed juice, served undiluted, but most of the time it's prohibitively expensive, so diluted juice from concentrate is the next best choice.

Milk is a great menu choice, because it provides both protein and calcium, which vulnerable people may not get enough of. Dairy is expensive, though, so budget carefully.

Be aware of potential allergens when creating your menu, especially if you're working with kids. I never use nuts in anything served in a school. Occasionally the food bank or some other donor will give us bread that contains nuts, in which case we give it to a family that needs it, but we never put it in the toaster. You don't want cross-contamination in your kitchen.

Use all of your leftovers! Choose menu items you can reuse, and be creative. Soup can be reheated, muffins and baked goods can be frozen and saved for another day, and fruit can be whizzed into delicious smoothies.

When setting up a menu, ask yourself the following questions:
- What type of menu should I offer?
- How will I make healthy food choices?
- How complicated does it need to be?
- What recipes should I use?
- How will we prepare the food?

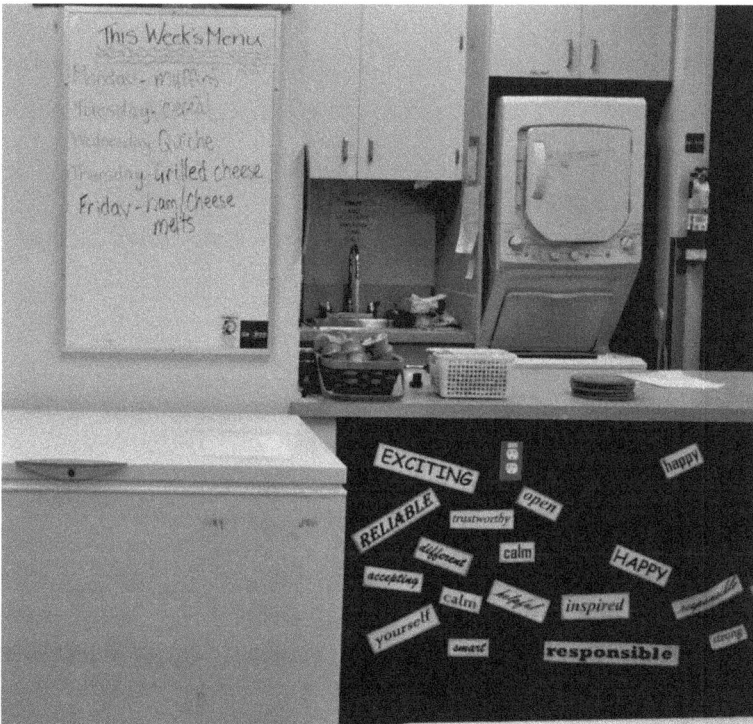

Type of Menu

One of the best and most cost-efficient plans for a meal program is a menu rotation—that is, a set of menus that you repeat in the same order, week after week.

In a one-week menu rotation, the meals are the same each week. Everyone knows what to expect on Tuesday. In a two-week rotation, you use one menu for the first week and a second menu for the second week, alternating the two menus over each two-week period. In a three-week rotation, the menu changes every week for three weeks, then starts over again in week four.

This system works with a four-week rotation, a five-week rotation, and so on. The longer the rotation, the more your clients will enjoy it and the less likely they are to tire of the menu choices.

A menu rotation helps keep you on budget and provides consistency for both your volunteers and your clients. It also keeps your clients interested. Knowing exactly what you'll serve each day and each week doesn't hurt you or your budget, and it provides your clients with variety. No one likes tedium. Even people who don't get enough to eat enjoy a varied menu, and a varied diet is healthier than a narrow diet. Some of your clients may even try foods they haven't had before.

If you only feel comfortable with a one-week rotation, it will work. Just be sure your meal choices are healthy.

Include two main menu choices for every meal. For breakfast, for example, you can offer a choice of a ham-and-cheese melt or a bowl of yogurt and granola.

Some people may ask for both options. This will cost more, so it's up to you whether to allow it. You can decide how open and flexible your program will be.

Plan your menus on a spreadsheet. This helps with planning and gives you an accurate week-by-week overview of your budget. Once you're up and running on a menu rotation, your food costs shouldn't change unless your clientele grows or shrinks.

You might prefer to create a new menu each week, especially if you're open only one day a week, or if you want to see how many food donations you'll receive before deciding what to serve. This will make your job a bit harder, and your food costs will change all the time. You'll have to purchase everything you need each week, then come up with recipes and make the meals. If this works for you, great. Create a system you're comfortable with.

If you want to run your program like a restaurant, making meals to order, you really have to think about logistics and food costs. You may end up with wasted food and added expense. Perhaps you can minimize this problem by partnering with a restaurant to operate a food truck. It's usually simpler and more cost-effective to serve a meal buffet-style, rather than cooking food to order.

Your weekly menu should be visible to everyone you serve. Write the day's main choices on a whiteboard where your clients line up, or display a sample meal, so they know what you're offering. You may end up with more clients if people can see that you'll be serving lasagna on Thursday! It gives people something to look forward to. Kids love reading the weekly menus and get excited when they see something they love to eat advertised.

Healthy Food Choices

I know you know this, but I have to say it: a burger with fries doesn't qualify as a healthy food choice. Neither does a stack of chocolate-chip pancakes. Beef burgers made in house with quinoa salad or whole-wheat blueberry pancakes are much healthier choices. You might think it's nice to offer burgers and fries or chocolate-chip pancakes as a special treat, but that's the wrong way to think.

French fries are not a vegetable! They're simply grease in stick form. Notice that there's no deep fryer on our list of kitchen appliances in Chapter 3.

You may have to ignore your emotions when choosing what to serve and think about how you can pack the most nutrients into your clients' bodies. Remember why you're creating this program. Is it to give people empty calories, or is it to provide the healthiest food choices you can within your budget?

Try not to get caught up with the notion of serving something "people will love." How do you know what they'll love? If they're already eating your healthy choices, why jeopardize that by giving them an unhealthy "treat" and making it acceptable? If you serve healthy food, they'll eat healthy food, because they're hungry.

A food program should teach people how to select balanced meals, promoting healthy choices and good table manners. Even some adults haven't been taught how to behave at a table, or don't know what a cucumber tastes like. Expand their minds and their palates. Acquaint them with foods they may never have tried, prepared in different ways.

If you're ever in doubt about what constitutes a healthy food choice, go online and look up "healthy food guide." It will give you many good ideas.

Healthy food choices aren't cheap. They usually cost more than cheaper foods, so factor this into your budget from the outset. This is important.

Healthy food choices help to reduce obesity, take pressure off the health-care system, and create a more productive community. Healthy people are happier and more productive than unhealthy people. They can think more clearly, and they often behave better. Isn't that what we want?

Keeping it Simple

Your clients are coming to eat what you serve. Don't feel that you have to cater to each person's preferences.

When making choices, I like the motto KISS—Keep It Simple, Shannah. I might offer diluted juice and water one day, milk and water the next, and so on. If you were to walk into a room where you were served a free meal, would you complain that there's no juice, or would you say nothing and grab the water or milk option? Would you complain that a wrap isn't a proper sandwich? I'm pretty sure you wouldn't say anything. You'd simply choose the option you like best and eat it.

Think of what *you* would do. Your clients are just like you, and ninety percent of the time they'll behave the way you do. Some of them have held good jobs and have simply fallen on hard times. Any of us could find ourselves in their shoes. You never know how life will unfold.

I've experienced hard times myself a couple of times. I had to use a food bank to feed my baby and myself when I was a young single mom. Many years later, I was divorced and making minimum wage, so I couldn't afford to get my kiddos anything for Christmas. For two years in a row I had to sign up for a Christmas hamper, and I went back to the food bank a few times.

I didn't look at what I was getting from these programs—I simply smiled and cried at the generosity shown to me during a difficult time. I was in survival mode. I knew I had to feed my boys, and I looked on any help with gratitude. It was a humbling experience, and I will always be thankful for the help I received when I was down.

You're doing a very good thing for the people who use your program. Even if they don't say anything, the fact that they keep coming back is rewarding. They *are* grateful . . . and probably a little embarrassed by the situation they find themselves in. Smile at them, ask them how they are, listen to what they say. You may be the only person in their day who treats them like this. Don't be offended if they don't answer you. One day they may open up.

Keeping things simple means putting every food item you're serving on every plate (unless it's an allergen). If someone doesn't like something, they won't eat it. You may think that's a waste of food, but someone may finally try that green thing on the plate and actually like it. Now look what you've done—you've introduced another healthy item into the diet of someone who needs it.

One time a little girl appeared in front of me, looked up at me with big brown eyes, and said in the most innocent voice, "Why did they put a tomato on my plate? I don't even like tomatoes. But I ate it."

"Do you like tomatoes now?" I asked.

"I guess so." She turned and skipped away.

Another child yelled across the room, "Is there zucchini in this cake?"

"Yes, there is," I called.

"I hate zucchini, but I love this!" he shouted. "I'm going to eat more zucchini more now. YUM!"

When people see other people eating things they'd normally never touch, those items can start to look appealing. If they're on their plate, too, they might take a bite.

Don't get too fancy. You don't need a garnish. You don't need to over-embellish the meal. You don't need to have four meal options. Keep it simple—one meal, one alternate choice, one drink. Cover the nutritional requirements in your meal, and serve it.

A common mistake is to over-think the menu. I've seen people become overwhelmed because their menus required too many prep and cooking steps. Simple, good, healthy recipes that use just a few steps will make your program a success.

Recipe Choices

Once you know what you're serving (breakfast, lunch, supper, snacks) and what type of program you're running (grab-and-go, sit-down, classroom, bagged, or take-home meals), you can choose appropriate recipes. The Internet is your best recipe source.

Look for simple recipes with healthy ingredients. I like to try new recipes at home first, then increase the ingredient amounts. When you magnify a recipe, it changes, so keep track of how much of each ingredient you use and whether you change any ingredient, so your new recipe will be accurate. You may need to experiment to get it just right. This is where it's helpful to work with someone who has a culinary background—they can help figure out what may be lacking in a recipe.

You can change recipes a bit to keep food costs down. In a recipe for bacon-and-cheddar muffins, for example, you can substitute a cheaper option like ham for the bacon, then reduce the cheddar by half. Reducing the flour isn't a good idea, because it alters the base recipe too much, but ham and cheese are additives to the base recipe.

You can also change recipes to make them more nutritious. You may be able to use unsweetened apple sauce in place of water, or substitute an olive-oil blend for butter or margarine. It may take a few tries to perfect a recipe, but once it works, it's yours. You've created a healthier option.

Remember that some ingredients produce a lot of liquid when they're cooked. If you add zucchini to a recipe, for instance, you need to eliminate some of the liquid the recipe calls for to compensate for the moisture the zucchini will produce during the cooking process.

Be prepared to show your recipe book to the public, whether the recipes are your own, someone else's, or downloaded from the Internet. Don't worry that someone will steal your recipes.

I once created a five-week, colour-coded menu rotation binder, with temperature guides and HACCP information on the back of each recipe. It looked impressive. Someone from a major organization came to my program, saw the binder, and suddenly had one of their own.

Before I even knew it was out there, people from other food programs came to me, upset, and said, "I can't believe they stole your binder!"

I replied, "Well, it's not cool that they did that without asking me, but I guess it's okay. If my binder helps this organization improve its food program, isn't that my main goal, anyhow?"

"Yes, but Shannah, you aren't generating any money off that."

"I know, but people are in need, and I want to help them."

In the long run, the information that organization provided to the programs it sponsored helped those programs succeed. Because of my information, those programs could run more effectively.

If someone from another meal program uses your ideas and recipes, be honoured. Your information can help provide greater access to healthy, enjoyable meals. Most people will ask before using your ideas and recipes, though. Most of us are respectful and play by the rules.

Food Preparation

Food preparation can be tricky. It all hinges on how much time you have for prep and cooking, how many people you're working with, what you're serving, and how many people you're feeding. You have to plan shifts and workflow so you'll have enough staff to serve the right items on the right days.

If kids come to your school breakfast program between eight o'clock and eight-thirty, for instance, your kitchen workers should begin before seven-thirty. This gives them thirty minutes to cook the food and get it ready to serve.

The best way to manage workflow is by using production sheets to plan the week's activities. A production sheet tells you what must be done to serve a meal on a particular day, as well as what prep must be done for the following days.

You have to manage kitchen time carefully—especially if it takes fifteen or twenty minutes to get the oven up to temperature. Spend money on an oven that will heat up in five minutes or less, and get a gas stove, if you can. You need to differentiate prep time from cooking time, know how long to allocate for each step, and fit those steps into the week's plan.

Lasagna, for example, takes a while to cook from scratch. You have to make the meat sauce (which can take thirty minutes to two hours, depending on the sauce), cook the noodles (thirty minutes), put the casserole together (twenty minutes), and bake it (one hour). That adds up to about four hours. However, if you make the sauce and cook the noodles one day, assemble the casserole the next day, and cook and serve it on the third day, you won't be overwhelmed.

You'll have a different production sheet in your binder for each day of your menu rotation. Each production sheet needs to be specific so your volunteers will know what to do.

Let's say you plan to serve pumpkin-spice pancakes to ninety kids on Thursday. The recipe is made from scratch with pumpkins, apple sauce, and eggs. Since it's challenging for two kitchen workers to make fresh pancakes for that many people in just thirty minutes, you'll use your production sheets to break the prep time into manageable chunks, like this:

- Tuesday's production sheet will say, "Make pancake batter. Cover, label, and date the bowl, and put it in the refrigerator."
- Wednesday's production sheet will say, "Cook pancakes on the griddle, then place them on parchment paper in a deep hotel pan. When they're cool, cut them up, cover, label, and date the pan, and put it in the refrigerator."

    (If you cut up the pancakes now, you won't have to wash a bunch of knives later. And anything served to kiddos should be bite-sized so they don't have to handle knives at all.)
- Thursday's production sheet will say, "When you come in, turn on the oven. Uncover the hotel pan full of pancakes and put it in the oven. When the pancakes are hot, remove the hotel pan from the oven and serve them."

If you're making banana bread, you can prepare the batter and pour it into a four-inch hotel pan lined with parchment paper on Monday, bake it on Tuesday, and slice and serve it on Wednesday.

If you plan to serve cereal with apple slices and an alternate choice of yogurt on Tuesday morning, banana bread on Wednesday, and pancakes on Thursday, your production sheet for Tuesday will look something like this:

Tuesday's Production Sheet

Set-Up
- o   Sign in.
- o   Turn on washing machine.
- o   Preheat the oven on to 175°C (350°F).
- o   Immediately put banana bake in oven.
- o   Put out the tables and chairs.
- o   Put out bowls, plates, coffee cups (if you're serving coffee), spoons, and napkins.
- o   Turn on coffee maker (for parents and volunteers).
- o   Put out milk and sugar for coffee.
- o   Empty dishwasher.
- o   Make pancake batter.
- o   Cover, label, and date pancake batter and put it in refrigerator.
- o   Cut apples into slices.
- o   Put out cereal, milk, and apple slices (main breakfast choice).
- o   Put out yogurt (alternate breakfast choice).
- o   Put out beverages.
- o   Check dryer, fold and put away the clean laundry.
- o   When banana bake is cooked, remove from oven to cool.
- o   When banana bread is cool, cover, label, and date it and put it in refrigerator.

Clean-Up
- o   Use disinfectant spray and a clean cloth to wipe down the tables.
- o   Put away the tables and chairs.
- o   Empty, clean, and refill the coffee machine.
- o   Count the used dishes and record the number of meals served on the client log sheet.
- o   Fill and turn on the dishwasher.
- o   Use a cloth to wash all of the sinks with soap and water, rinsing them clean.

o   Use disinfectant spray and a clean cloth to wipe down the countertops.

o   Make sure all of the appliances are unplugged and that the oven and stove elements are turned off.

o   Transfer wet laundry into the dryer and put all of the used towels and cloths into the washing machine.

o   Sign out. Thank you!

Chapter 6

Sourcing Ingredients

In an ideal world, we'd consume our food within a few hours of harvesting it ourselves from organic gardens. People using food programs could help harvest the ingredients for the program meals, then take home any extra food they've picked.

It's not just a daydream. Some organizations have started growing their own food in greenhouses built specifically for their meal programs. Unless you have your own farm, though, you need to determine where you'll get the food for your program.

Do you want to help your community by purchasing locally, and perhaps pay more for it? Do you want to work with a company that delivers the food to your facility, so you don't have to worry about holding temperatures during transport? Do you want to shop around for the best prices?

Each decision you make now will create the foundation for your program, so make your choices carefully. When sourcing ingredients, ask yourself the following questions:

- How will you transport and store the food?
- Are there ways to make ordering easier?

- Should you join forces with other meal programs?
- Should you work with a food bank or another organization?
- Should you ask the local community for help?

Food Transportation and Storage

It's critical that food be transported and stored at the correct holding temperatures, so harmful bacteria can't begin to grow.

Whoever picks up the food for your program must take it directly from the store to your facility. Once the food's in the car, there's no stopping for coffee, and no running into the store for "just one item." We all know how long that can take. It's easy to get distracted and forget about the food in your car. If it's hot outside, food that requires refrigeration will start to spoil the moment it leaves the store, so you must take this seriously. The food must go directly from point A to point B, with no stopping in between.

Some grocery stores will deliver smaller orders in refrigerated trucks. This eliminates the potential for improper storage.

Using a service like this might mean you can't look around for the best deal, though, and you can buy only what the store has available. There may also be a delivery fee. The store may be willing to waive the fee—and perhaps give you a discount on your purchases—if you order regularly, especially if your program helps the store fulfill its community-service goals.

If you're thinking of bypassing your local grocery store and going directly to a major food distributor, there are things you should know. First, unless you spend at least $500 a month (the minimum charge for most distributors), a major food distributer is unlikely to deliver the products directly to you. And second, if you do purchase that much food, you'll need a lot of storage space. Buying in bulk is great for getting the best prices, but it can cause other problems if you have limited space.

Ordering

Ordering for a kitchen is pretty much the same no matter what type of menu you offer. If you're on a menu rotation and you have a set of standardized ordering sheets, you'll always know what to buy and the process will go smoothly.

Once you've decided on your menu rotation, use it to create a set of weekly ordering sheets. This will save you and your staff a lot of time later. It's how restaurants and commercial kitchens typically operate.

1. Write down everything you'll need for the first week. Go through each recipe and list all of the ingredients for each one.
2. Categorize all of your items under headings such as "Dry Goods," "Dairy," "Meat," "Produce," and "Other." Don't forget non-food items, such as plastic wrap, resealable plastic bags, and dishwasher detergent.
3. Place a triple underscore or box next to each item where you can write the quantity you need as you use the sheet. For example, if you have 3 jugs of milk in your inventory and you need 5 you would write down "2 jugs" beside "Milk" in order to make up the 5 jugs.
4. Label the sheet "Week 1."
5. Do the same to create a sheet for each subsequent week in your menu rotation.
6. Create a set of copies for your binder.

Week 1

MEAT
____ 1 toupie ham

DAIRY
____ 5 (4-litre/1-gallon) jugs whole (homogenized) milk
____ 2 (500-gram/17.6-ounce) containers cream cheese
____ 1 dozen eggs

___ 1 large tub margarine

___ 4 large tubs vanilla yogurt (NOT plain yogurt)

___ 1 large bag shredded cheddar cheese

PRODUCE

___ 3 English cucumbers

___ 25 bananas

___ 12 oranges

___ 11 apples

___ 1 (453-gram/1-pound) bag carrots

___ 4 (1-litre/1-quart) containers orange or apple juice

___ 1 bottle lemon juice

BREAD AND CEREAL

___ 5 loaves whole-grain bread

___ 1 loaf gluten-free bread (or more, depending on how many gluten-sensitive clients you have)

___ 4 dozen whole-grain buns

___ 1 dozen gluten-free buns (or more, depending on how many gluten-sensitive clients you have)

___ 2 jumbo boxes Rice Krispies (which are naturally gluten-free)

___ 1 jumbo box Shreddies

___ 1 jumbo box Corn Flakes

___ 1 jumbo box Cheerios

___ 1 (900-gram/32-ounce) bag gluten-free quick-cooking rolled oats

___ 6 bags bran muffin mix

CANNED GOODS

___ 1 (3-kilogram/106-ounce) can fruit salad

STAPLES

___ 1 (3-kilogram/6.6-pound) container liquid honey

___ 1 (1-kilogram/2.2-pound) container creamed honey

___ 2 (1-litre/1-quart) jars strawberry or raspberry jam

___ 1 (1-litre/1-quart) container vegetable oil (to blend with olive oil)

___ 1 (1-litre/1-quart) bottle extra-virgin olive oil (to blend with vegetable oil)

___ 1 large can cooking spray

___ 1 (1-litre/1-quart) bottle vanilla

___ 1 (5-kilogram/11-pound) bag unbleached flour

___ 1 (2.5-kilogram/5.5-pound) bag whole wheat flour

___ 1 (1-kilogram/2.2-pound) bag brown or golden-yellow sugar

___ 1 (1-kilogram/2.2-pound) container icing sugar

___ 1 (1.5-kilogram/3.3-pound) bag of white sugar

___ 1 (454-gram/8-ounce) container of baking soda

___ 1 (450-gram/8-ounce) container baking powder

___ 1 (680-gram/8-ounce) container cinnamon

___ 1 (45-gram/1.5-ounce) container ground nutmeg

___ 1 (45-gram/1.5-ounce) container allspice

___ 1 (45-gram/1.5-ounce) container ground cloves

DRY GOODS

___ 3 boxes large ziplock freezer bags

___ 2 boxes medium ziplock freezer bags

___ 2 rolls parchment paper

___ 1 roll plastic wrap (e.g., Saran Wrap, Glad Wrap)

___ 1 roll aluminum foil

___ 6 rolls paper towels

___ 5,000 napkins

CLEANING SUPPLIES

___ 1 (3-litre/102-ounce) bottle liquid dish soap

___ 90 portions dishwasher detergent

___ 5 large bottles hand sanitizer

___ 1 (3.78-litre/128-ounce) bottle multi-surface cleaner and disinfectant

___ 12 dish cloths or cleaning cloths

____   12 dish towels

____   3 sponges with scrubbies

____   1 apron per person

When you're ready to place an order, select the appropriate ordering sheet and customize it by writing the quantity you need next to each item. If your staff uses a white board in the kitchen to note items that are running low, use this information to complete your sheet. You can then take your customized list to the store, or use it to place an order online.

It's best to order your ingredients a week before you'll need them. Check with your supplier to be sure everything is in stock, and arrange for an appropriate delivery date.

Try to build an inventory of nonperishable items. You don't want to run out of anything before an order arrives.

Working with Other Food Programs

Consider working together with other food programs. You and the other organizers can brainstorm about what does and doesn't work, share recipes, and—most importantly—increase your buying power.

When you buy in bulk, you get lower prices. Major distributors typically require hefty minimum purchases, which can be out of your price range. By teaming up with other programs, you can place larger orders and meet those minimum requirements.

When you place a joint order, the food will most likely be delivered to one place. It needs to be split up there and transported to the other program sites. You and your fellow organizers can take turns having it delivered to you, or you can set up a regular routine where it's always delivered to a particular site and the rest of you retrieve it from there.

The ability to share resources in an emergency is another good reason to work with other meal programs. If you suddenly find that your major funder can no longer support you, for example, your partners in the other programs may be able to help out until you find another source of funding. If one program finds itself in a bind, the others can help by sharing food, resources, and even volunteers.

Getting Food Donations

Look for other organizations to help you. It can be a huge relief to feel supported by someone else. Another organization may be able to provide supplies, volunteers, funding, and/or advice. If they've invested in your program, they want you to succeed and will do their best to help if you're struggling.

Food Banks

Approach your local food bank about working together. It can be an excellent resource for your program. Because your target clients are the same, you can advertise for one another. The people who run the food bank can tell you a lot about the needs of the vulnerable people in your community. They may also be able to provide you with food.

A friend of mine arranged for her high school to receive a portion of her local food bank's overstocked baked goods. This helped with her program's budget, and she even had enough bread products to share some with a program I was running. She was able to distribute perishable food that would have otherwise gone to waste *and* help the food bank reach more of its target demographic.

When people go to a food bank, they take the food home and cook it themselves. Once a week, most of these people are given enough food for just two days. That's not enough for a whole week, but it's a start. It's meant to supplement what they already have at home, which isn't always very nutritious. By directing them to your program, the food bank can provide its clients with extra meal support.

Grocery Stores

Grocery stores can be wonderful partners for your meal program. Some stores will provide gift cards. Some will give you discounts on items you order often. Some will donate products for your program. Most grocery stores want to be seen as leaders who contribute to their communities.

You might ask for weekly donations of bread products or of fruits and vegetables. Food donations are as good as money.

Farms

Local farms are wonderful sources of food—and farmers are usually community-minded. If you're lucky enough to live near a farming community, call some of the farms and make appointments to meet with them. You'll be surprised at how many different types of farms there are! Introduce yourself, tell them what you hope to accomplish, and ask whether they can help.

Many farmers will be pleased to help you, either by supplying produce at discounted rates or by offering occasional donations. A farmer once donated thirty pounds of frozen blueberries and thirty pounds of frozen strawberries to a program I ran. We used them in muffins, smoothies, and loafs. The berries lasted for a long time and saved us a ton of money.

Involving the Local Community

Think about other organizations you might be able to work with.

Can you partner with a local hardware or drugstore, offering advertising in exchange for supplies? Can a local service club or church help you find volunteers or funding as part of its commitment to community service?

Think about how you and other organizations can both benefit from a partnership, then approach them about working together. You never know who will say yes, or what good ideas they might have.

The first time I started a food program, I asked every store in the neighbourhood for a donation. Once the kitchen was up and running, I used word of mouth to advertise the program. Then I invited community members to volunteer or to observe the program.

This last thing turned out to be a key factor in the program's success. I invited everyone I could reach—church members, restaurant managers, grocery store owners, politicians, newspaper people, and more. Mine became the most successful program around because of all the support it received.

It also helped that I listened to the suggestions of community volunteers and observers. They gave me valuable information about who to talk to, how to cut costs, and where to apply for more grants.

Listen to your community members. Involve them. Consider their suggestions, even if you don't agree with them at first. Perhaps a small tweak to an odd-sounding suggestion will result in a great idea. Or a suggestion might be useful down the road. Don't discount anything.

Taking people's advice can make them feel more connected to your program and make them want to support it even more.

Growing Your Own Food

Having access to a community garden or local farmland to grow your own food could offset some of your food costs and provide healthy, organic produce for your program.

Some of your clients may enjoy helping to tend the garden as volunteers. This can get them out into the fresh air, give them purpose, and teach them a new life skill. Many people find it both calming and empowering to get their hands into the earth and nurture green growth—something marginalized people may not often experience.

You can create a productive little garden even if you don't have access to a farm. If you have enough sunlight and a water source, you can make a garden almost anywhere. I've seen parking lots transformed into lovely community gardens with raised garden beds and containers.

Chapter 7

Staying Within a Budget

Budgeting is never easy . . . but try feeding breakfast to eighty kids a day, five days a week for a whole school year on a budget of $800 a month. That works out to around fifty cents per meal per child, with only volunteers running your program. Can you provide healthy food choices for that amount?

Yes, and no. It is possible to run a nutritious food program that your clients will like without spending a huge amount. You need to plan carefully, though. Organize your resources and create a set of cost-effective, nutritious menus. Figure out your budget, and stick to it—no crazy splurging, overpaying people, or overfeeding people.

(Figuring out your budget means looking at the types of meals you're serving and whether you have any paid employees, monitoring your local food and supply costs, and knowing what types of donations and other funding sources you can count on.)

You might think it would be a nice treat to substitute bacon for ham if you find the bacon on sale. But it may still be cheaper to purchase a toupie ham (a ham that's been processed to remove the bone and muscle, then shaped into a smooth oval) and cutting it up yourself. I can get three meals for eighty kids out of one $20 toupie ham or out of six $4 packages of bacon. The ham is $4 cheaper, even though the bacon is on sale.

You might argue that bacon and ham aren't the healthiest choices, but they are proteins people are familiar with. You can use them at first and build up your clients' trust before you move them toward healthier options. And when you're working on a tight budget, it may be challenging to offer higher quality choices when you first start your program.

If you can cut costs without compromising nutritional value or your clients' health, go ahead and scale down. Sometimes it might be hard, and you may want to throw your hands up and say, "To heck with it! Today I'm just going to get the two-percent milk, because they're all out of whole [homogenized] milk." You've just doubled your cost. (As we'll see later in the chapter, you can dilute whole milk by fifty percent, but you won't want to do that with two-percent milk.)

Stick to your program and your values, and you should be able to stay on task and on budget.

To stay within your budget, ask yourself the following questions:
- Who might donate equipment and supplies?
- How can I spend less?
- How can I control food waste?
- Can I use volunteers?
- How can I make the program financially sustainable for the long term?

Equipment and Supply Donations

The more equipment you can start with, the easier your life will be. A fully equipped kitchen will help things run smoothly and keep morale high.

There's nothing wrong with asking a local store to donate small items such as griddles, blenders, utensils, plates, and pots and pans.

You can start with a phone call to the store manager. Explain that you're running a meal program and need a few small items to help the program run better.

Some stores ask that charitable requests be put in writing. Your letter should state exactly what you're asking for and how you'll use it. Use your program's letterhead, or see if you can use that of your hosting facility. You'll find a sample letter you can modify for your own use in Appendix F.

It's often easier to get donations when you can offer tax receipts. To offer tax receipts, your organization must have a tax number, or at least be a member of another organization that has a tax number. If you can offer tax receipts, include this information in your letter.

Make your requests very specific. I once asked for a large KitchenAid mixer without specifying the exact size I needed. The store generously donated one that was smaller than we wanted. It did make our lives easier, but instead of making one batch of zucchini loaf batter, we had to make two. Still, it was better than using a whisk and arm power!

Be smart with your requests. Ask specific stores for specific items, then follow up with phone calls to see if they're willing to help. Don't ask multiple stores for the same items—you don't want to end up with twelve sets of pots and pans! There's nothing worse than having to return a donation that you asked for in the first place.

Grocery stores may be willing to donate food items and cleaning supplies. Some will provide gift cards on a regular basis, while others may prefer to make large single donations.

As I mentioned in Chapter 6, your local food bank may be able to provide food items, depending on what it has available. By giving us some of the bread products they'd received from local stores, our food bank helped us save thousands of dollars over the school year. They worked with us because doing so helped fill vulnerable kids' tummies.

Why not ask your local restaurants if they'll donate food to your program, or perhaps even help with cooking? I know of a wonderful fine-dining restaurant that served a catered dinner for people in a local meal program, and everyone loved it. It happens. All you have to do is ask.

Spending Less

Start by taking a month's worth of receipts—not your start-up month, but a month from when your program is up and running—and make a list of all the products you've purchased. Now tally up how much you've spent on each item. By figuring out what you've spent the most on and tapering your costs for those items, you'll start to save money.

Dairy and meat will be your biggest expenses.

We were spending way too much on milk. Our recipes for cereal, baked goods, pancake mixes, and hot chocolate all called for milk. So I tried different things to cut down, such as serving milk less often.

Then, as if an apple had dropped on my head, I thought of buying higher-fat milk and diluting it with water. We were already diluting juice by fifty percent to reduce the sugar content, so why not dilute milk by fifty percent, too? We could use that in smoothies, hot chocolate, and baked goods.

It didn't taste bad at all.

I did struggle with the idea at first, because I didn't want to limit the kids' calcium intake. Then I realized that diluting whole (homogenized) milk (which is 3.25 percent milk fat) by half would be almost the same as giving them 2-percent milk. It would be healthier, too, because there's less sugar in diluted 3.25-percent milk.

We started using the diluted milk in cereal and baking, and continued to serve the undiluted 3.25-percent milk for drinking, to keep up the calcium intake.

Next, I tried serving undiluted milk and water one day, just water the next day, and diluted juice and water the day after that, alternating the choices for a week. It was a defining moment. I discovered that many people are happy with plain water as a beverage option, which meant I didn't have to buy as much milk and juice.

By going over the bills and targeting the highest costs, I was able to develop other money-saving techniques. If a recipe called for three cups of shredded cheese, for example, I found that I could cut it down to two cups, or sometimes even a cup and a half, depending on what I was making.

Use your common sense and modify your recipes to save money. Just be careful not to compromise too much on nutrition. Look for no-name brands, buy in bulk whenever you can, and watch for sales.

Reducing Waste

The easiest way to save money in a kitchen is by controlling food costs. It's not enough to limit your spending. You also have to avoid waste.

Salvage and repurpose your leftovers. If you open a four-litre can of fruit, for example, strain and freeze whatever you don't need and use it later in smoothies, muffins, or baked goods. Use your vegetable trimmings and meat scraps to make soup. Almost every part of a vegetable or meat item can be used in soup or stock or another meal.

Organization and rotation are key to keeping food costs down. Put your leftovers into freezer bags, label them with the date and contents, and freeze them. Keep everything you'll use for soup in the same part of the freezer.

Rotate your stock, using older products first. There's nothing worse than having to throw away food because you used newer products while older products went bad.

By controlling my food costs, I can make breakfast pancakes from scratch (containing eggs, apple sauce, and milk) and serve them with pure maple syrup, fruit salad, and the option of milk, juice, or water for just thirty cents a person. Serving pancakes once a week significantly cuts my food costs and helps my budget. I serve healthier breakfasts on the other days of the week, for balanced nutrition. This brings the cost up to about fifty cents per person per meal. This breakfast may be the only meal my clients will get in a day, so I try to make it nutritious.

Working with Volunteers

As we discussed in Chapter 4, you can save money by recruiting volunteers as well as paid employees.

People who volunteer are typically very committed. Unfortunately, many also have day jobs and may have to reduce their volunteer hours at times. And some simply don't show up. They may save you money, but relying on volunteers can be tricky.

You'll therefore need at least one paid employee with culinary experience. As a professional chef, I can run a small program myself, though for a larger program, I need help with prep, cooking, and cleaning. If you hire someone with culinary experience, you won't need as many people in the kitchen. And someone with experience will know how to order efficiently and keep food costs down, as well as how to direct the kitchen volunteers in a positive way.

Building Sustainability

To be sustainable, your program needs renewable funding. When applying for grants, ask whether you can negotiate two-, three-, or even ten-year renewable contracts.

Seeing is believing. Why not ask your sponsors to come and help serve meals for a shift, or simply to come and observe? This will help them feel connected to your program. If they can see the difference their generosity makes, they may be motivated to continue funding you even if their money becomes tight down the road and they have to cut something from their spending.

I once had the kids in my program draw breakfast pictures, then sent them to our sponsors with thank-you notes. This made their financial support personal. The sponsors loved it.

Your program should include some kind of public recognition of your sponsors. When they come to visit, let them see that you have acknowledged and publicized their generosity.

Making new connections and keeping the community involved will build awareness of how badly needed your program is. Invite local businesspeople to come by and help for a shift. Ask the mayor and other officials to help serve a meal and invite the local newspaper to send a photographer.

Networking is key to your success. Every connection you make is another person who wants your program to succeed. If a backer becomes unable to support your program, someone else in your network may be able to help. You must build a strong network of connections. If you're not comfortable doing this, find someone who is.

Always send thank-you letters to the people who support your program, whether they provide funding, volunteer their time, or help spread the word. People who feel valued will continue to support you.

Chapter 8

Funding the Program

You may wonder why we've waited this long to talk about funding. Shouldn't it come first?

Yes, obviously, you should have the funding in place before you launch your program. But you need to decide on the type of program your community needs, where you'll situate it, who will do the work, what you'll serve, and where you'll get your ingredients before you'll know how much it will all cost.

Funding is available from a variety of sources. You can raise money with the help of any and all of the following:

- Sponsors
- Grants
- Fundraising events
- User fees or donations

Sponsors

Coming up with the money to start a food program isn't that difficult. Most people will see the need once you explain the problem. Everyone knows what it feels like to be hungry, and that's a blessing of sorts for you. Everyone understands the need for regular meals.

When you begin looking for sponsors, you may be over-whelmed by the generosity your program receives. Society has an aversion to seeing people go hungry, so you're likely to have plenty of sponsors offering their money or time. The dilemma will be funding the program on a continuing basis, year after year. People's financial circumstances—and their focus of attention—can change.

You therefore need renewable contracts. You want your program to run successfully for years, until it's (hopefully) no longer needed. Renewable contracts will help with this.

Showcase your sponsors. Give them the recognition they deserve! A sign on the wall or a billboard at the door thanking your sponsors will make them happy when they visit. They'll love to see that their money is going to a good cause, and this may encourage them to renew your contracts each year.

Two excellent sources of sponsorship are churches and local businesses.

Religious Organizations

Churches, mosques, temples, synagogues, and other religious institutions are wonderful resources for meal programs. Most faith-based groups are community oriented and want to help when they see a need. If you go to a congregation and explain the circumstances, the people are likely to help any way they can.

Asking for a donation from the group is a good start. The congregation may even want to take the program on itself.

I know of a school breakfast program where that's exactly what happened. The program coordinator made it clear that church members were not to preach their religion to the kids, and it worked out well. The school administrators were pleased that the kids were fed, and the church members were happy to help.

If you're running a secular program, especially if it involves a school, you must make it clear what the rules are. You can make it known that the church is funding and/or staffing the program, but you need to emphasize the need to keep religion out of conversations with your clients, if that's what you want.

If you belong to a church that wants to start its own meal program, it's up to you whether religious conversations are to be part of the program. It depends on what you're trying to achieve. If your main goal is to feed people, rather than to convert them, keeping religious talk to a minimum will make the program more inviting for those who aren't religious or who follow a different faith than yours.

If you do wish to include religion in your meal program, address this with your funders right up front and make sure they're okay with it. A church in my city ran a food program that turned away people who weren't accepting of that denomination. Its program lost its government funding because it didn't serve everyone. If you want to reach people, you may need to invite them all in, without discriminating.

Your church probably has some funds in place, but you may want to solicit donations from other groups to help with your start-up costs.

Businesses

Local businesses are also good places to look for sponsorships.

Some companies like to get involved with community programs, and your meal program could be just what they're looking for. Approach a few businesses in your area and tell them about your program. Explain the need you're trying to meet and give them a ballpark figure for your yearly financial requirements.

If you find cold calling difficult, sit down ahead of time and write down what you want to say. If a company can donate even a small amount, that will be wonderful!

If they don't say yes right away, ask them to think about it and say you'll drop off an information letter, so they can be fully informed.

Then hand deliver a letter printed on the letterhead of the facility you plan to use. Tug on their heartstrings! Explain why you're starting this program, why there's a need for it, where it will be, how much money you hope to raise this year, what the money will fund, and how much it will cost to keep the program running year after year. Include your contact information, your phone number, and the name and phone number of someone of authority in your facility, whether it's a school, a church, a community centre, or what have you. Be transparent.

After you deliver your heartfelt letter, follow up with a phone call. Always follow up with a phone call! If they're still unsure, ask them to take their time thinking about it and say you'll be in touch. Give them up to a month, then call again to see if they've made a decision.

Your program may take a while to get started, especially if you're installing a kitchen, so waiting for funds from one company won't be a huge issue at first.

Grants

Search the Internet for organizations that offer grants to help fund your meal program.

If you can't find someone offering a grant in your area, do some digging. From my home in Greater Vancouver, I applied for grants from organizations as far north as Nunavut and as far east as Ontario. The program I ran was fortunate enough to receive a three-year renewable contract from the Breakfast Club of Canada and yearly grants from Breakfast for Learning.

If you can secure a renewable grant, you may breathe a sigh of relief, but don't rely on it entirely. A grant should fund only a portion of your program. You need to keep raising money. Advocate for funds from other sources, in case something happens to your grant.

If you lose a grant and you have other sources of funds, your program will still be able to run, even if you have to scale it down to bare bones for a while. Something is always better than nothing.

Meeting Funders' Requirements

If your program is partly funded by a grant, especially if it comes from a food organization, you must be respectful and follow the organization's nutritional guidelines.

Most organizations that sponsor food programs want you to distribute the food in particular ways. They might specify how many days a week you can serve juice, for example, or the nutritional content your meals should provide.

Such requirements are usually intended to make sure the grant money is funding healthy choices. They often come with nutritional guidelines, recipes, and/or menu ideas, which can help you plan your program.

Your funding organization can often offer support, too, if you need it. It's nice to be able to call someone to ask what to do next, if you're stuck. Setting up a program can be a bit overwhelming at first, and having someone to talk to is reassuring.

Most funding organizations also ask for your financial reports. Don't let yourself get behind on these! If you don't stay on top of your reports, your funding may be withheld.

You'll be asked to indicate how much you've received in donations, whether in cash or in kind, as well as how many hours your volunteers have given. Keep all of your receipts. Have your volunteers log their in and out times in a sign-in book. (You'll find a sample sign-in sheet in Appendix F—Personnel Forms.)

You'll also be asked how many people you serve each month, so find a way to count them. You might count the dirty plates, have your clients take tickets from a dispenser, or even ask them to move a token from one container to another each time they have a meal. You need something tangible that you can count.

Your funding organization may want to highlight your program as an example of its work. It might ask for on-site recognition of its sponsorship in the form of posters, signage, aprons, stickers, or whatever it sends you for display. It might even want to send its sponsors to volunteer with your program. I like to call these people cameo volunteers, because they come once or twice, help out for a shift, and see their organization's presence in your program. Even if it's covering only fifty percent of your budget, the organization is an integral part of your program and should be prominently acknowledged.

Fundraising Events

Fundraisers are excellent ways to raise money. They take time to organize, and they require volunteers, so be sure you have committed people lined up!

Fundraisers can take many forms. I've helped raise money through pub nights, Grand Prix racing galas, film festivals, banquets, car washes, bottle drives, craft fairs, golf tournaments, and carnivals.

The most successful fundraising events have more than one revenue stream. In addition to selling entry tickets, they might include silent auctions, 50/50 draws, and door prizes.

I know of one foundation that held a golf tournament and raised $80,000 for several school food programs. This was enough to fund one school's breakfast program, serving up to ninety students a day, for eight years! The foundation has done this for several years in a row, funding a variety of meal programs in the community.

A Nonprofit Foundation

The more legitimate your program seems, the more people will attend your fundraisers and make donations, especially for a cause such as feeding at-risk children and families. You might therefore think about creating a nonprofit foundation to handle the money.

A foundation shows that your program is legitimate. It generates trust, especially if your program isn't yet up and running. A foundation also gives you a tax number, so you can pay lower taxes on supplies and issue tax receipts for donations.

If you hope to launch multiple programs over time, or if you're planning to launch a program within a school, working through a foundation can improve your efficiency and help with any legal issues you may encounter.

Creating a foundation involves several legal steps. You need to form a board of directors, draft a set of bylaws, develop a strategic plan, establish accounting and record-keeping systems, file for local, regional, and federal tax exemptions, and meet government requirements for charitable organizations.

Contact the government and look on the Internet for information about how to start a nonprofit foundation.

User Fees or Donations

Although you'd probably rather avoid this, asking some of your program's clients for donations is another way to help with funding.

Some schools open their meal programs to every child and ask for small monthly fees or donations, while making sure the vulnerable kids never have to pay.

Presenting a fee as an optional donation ensures that there's no pressure on the parents whose kids genuinely need the program. Meanwhile, parents who are better off are less likely to feel guilty, because they're helping to pay the way rather than taking resources from needy children. If donations are optional, there's no stigma for anyone.

I know a woman to takes her son and his friend to a program that charges five dollars at the door for supper every Friday night. Several families attend this program. It's a regular night out for the kids with their families. They offer up board games for the clients to play and even have local musicians play live music there at times.

Meal programs offered through religious organizations, community centres, and other facilities have different clienteles from those in schools. They're typically not as diverse. People who come to community programs really need them. You don't see many young, middle-class couples on dates at community food programs! I therefore recommend that you keep your program virtually free for everyone who shows up. You can suggest that when they're on their feet again, they might like to make a donation to help others who still need the program. If you're running a daily program, consider setting up a money jar or some kind of donation station for those who can pay a little.

I knew a mom who was finally doing better after several years of hard financial struggle. The school had been so good to her child, helping out in their time of need, that she wanted to give something back. So she organized and paid for a full breakfast one morning, complete with hashbrowns, eggs, bacon, and toast. The lineup was out the door! Her child felt like royalty that day, because everyone knew his mom had supplied the meal. At one point during the meal we announced it was donated by him and his mom, and he stood up and threw his arms in the air with pride. It was a beautiful moment.

Chapter 9

Evaluating Your Program . . . and Spreading the Word

You've launched your program and it's been running for a month. Now you need to assess how it's doing.

Are there things you could do better? Things that are working well, and that you don't want to disrupt? Are you reaching the people who need your help?

As you gain more experience and get to know your clients, you'll find ways to make the program run more smoothly. You'll also find ways to help other groups set up their own programs.

Evaluating Your Program

Your success depends on regular self-evaluation and a willingness to make any necessary changes.

Every few months, look at all of the following to see if you can make improvements:

- Your kitchen procedures
- Your food costs
- The nutritional content of your menu selections
- Your service model

Kitchen Procedures

Take stock of how the kitchen appliances operate and make any necessary adjustments to your procedures. If you find that the oven takes a long time to heat up, for example, you'll need to turn it on at the beginning of each shift so the temperature is ready when you are.

Is your blender a bit small? Start blending smoothies as soon as you can, and put them in juice jugs so you don't get behind. Keep them in the refrigerator until you serve them. Smoothies usually separate when they're left to sit, so stir them before serving.

Can you prepare certain items the day before and leave them in the refrigerator? Making pancake batter the day before—especially if you make it from scratch—can be a big help when you have to pour and flip 300 pancakes in a hurry. For some items, such as a loaf, you can make the batter one day, bake it the next day, and serve the loaf the day after that.

Ask your staff for their ideas. You might be surprised at what they've noticed that you haven't.

Food Costs

Keep your eyes on your food costs. Small changes here can have a big impact on the success of your program.

Some organizations want receipts for everything their grants pay for. And some will reduce your grant next year if you don't spend your full allotment this year. This can be a problem if you receive more food donations than usual, or if you know your clientele isn't yet up to its full numbers. If you think you'll have grant money left over at the end of the year, use it to purchase dry goods and other nonperishable items such as flour, sugar, baking powder, spray oil, canned goods, and one-litre juice boxes.

Some grants can be used for non-food items, such as cooking utensils, appliances, and dishes. You therefore need to know all the details of your grant, including how you can spend the funds.

You, your program coordinator, or your paperwork coordinator must keep the books up to date and examine them every month to avoid going over budget. There's nothing worse than trying to pay a food bill only to find that the funds aren't there.

Healthy Food Choices

Are you serving the healthiest food choices? Are there better options?

Look at your recipes. Can you add or replace something to make them healthier?

If a recipe calls for water, for example, perhaps you can use milk instead. If a recipe includes sugar, think about replacing it with apple sauce or honey. Add zucchini to a chocolate cake batter or red lentils to spaghetti sauce for extra vitamins, minerals, and fibre.

There are many creative ways to make a meal healthier without your clients knowing about it. This is especially important for people who don't get—or don't like to eat—their recommended daily quota of fruits and vegetables.

Remember, this may be some people's only real meal of the day. Pack it with nutrition!

Service Model

How do you serve your clients? Is there a way to use your space more efficiently, or run your program more effectively?

Your clients may be happy to line up outside on warm summer days, for example, but what happens when it's cold and wet? Is there a sheltered area where they can sit and eat?

Do your clients know where to put their dirty dishes when they're finished eating? You may need a volunteer to make sure everyone knows where everything is.

If you find that you're getting fewer—or more—people than expected, think about changing your operating hours. Do you need to expand your days? Reduce them? Do you need to market your program better?

Be prepared to change your program on a regular basis until it becomes what you want it to be. You'll probably have to adapt your kitchen, storage, and serving areas, making changes as you figure out what works best. Most meal programs change quite a bit after they're launched.

Marketing Your Program

Your program will not succeed without good marketing. You have to reach out to the people you wish to serve and tell them how they can benefit from your program.

When you're getting started, you might consider a soft opening, where you advertise to a few people at first and let awareness spread through word of mouth. As more people hear about your program, more will come. This will bring clients in gradually, so you're not inundated by hordes of people who are curious and excited. It will also give you a manageable head count. A soft opening is a good approach for a school program.

If you prefer full exposure right away, you'll have to advertise widely. Spread the word by leaving flyers in unemployment offices, welfare offices, food banks, churches, libraries, schools, and medical buildings. Tell the local social workers what you're doing. If you're serving a school, use the school's public address system to invite students to participate in the program. Use social media to spread the word, inviting your target audience to come and see what you can do for them.

This more aggressive approach will help you reach more people than a soft opening will. It could, however, leave you overwhelmed with large numbers of clients before you're ready for them. Think carefully about your timing. You don't want to run out of food!

Target the Clients You Want

An effective marketing plan targets the specific clients you want to attract. You must identify your chosen demographic, finding out where they are and what resources are available to them. Then piggyback your marketing efforts on those resources.

If you cater to single mothers, for example, ask organizations that support single mothers to give your flyers to their clients. If you want to feed homeless people, go to the areas where they live and talk to them directly about your program. You might want to do this with a friend or colleague, for moral support as well as safety. Ask the local police and social workers to help spread the word. Most beat cops spend their days with homeless people and will be glad to steer them to a meal program.

If you're trying to reach a generalized low-income demographic, you might have better success by putting up posters and advertising on social media. Advertise a grand opening and invite everyone in your community. This may bring people out of hidden pockets of poverty and into your program.

Make it Safe

Simply making people aware of your program is not enough, though. You have to make it feel safe, so your clients are comfortable coming to you.

Can you include events after the food is served, such as games nights, poetry nights, or amateur nights? Many vulnerable people are lonely and will enjoy a chance to socialize with their peers after a good meal.

Be sure your marketing includes details about who is welcome. If people are invited to make donations, say so. If they're welcome even if they can't pay anything, say that, too. People need to know what to expect so they're not embarrassed when they arrive or upset that they can't partake.

And, as I've said above, reevaluate all aspects of your program every few months. It's the best way to catch things you haven't noticed before.

Helping Other Programs

There may come a day when other organizations want to follow in your footsteps. They may ask for your help in starting their own programs.

When I started my first breakfast program, I went to a few schools to see what they were doing and how they functioned. I asked about their contacts, their suppliers, their budgets, what they served, how they got volunteers, and whether I could call them with further questions. The program coordinators were great, answering my long list of questions.

We're all here for the same reason—to feed people in need. Once your program gets known, especially if it's a good one, you may start to get a lot of foot traffic observing your program and asking what you're doing.

My first breakfast program developed such an amazing reputation that observers from many organizations came to see how I was doing things. My program had a full-page story in the newspaper and was featured in a Breakfast Club of Canada video. I offered my Breakfast Club binder to anyone who asked to see it, recipes and all, because I wanted them all to succeed.

Each program is different. If you're asked for your expertise, don't be upset if the other program doesn't use the information you provide. It may not work for them, or the program coordinator may feel that it's just not something they can do.

By helping or collaborating with other programs, you may be able to combine your food purchases and buy in bulk for cheaper prices. You may also be able to share items that people have donated. If another program has been given a food processor, but already has one, it may send the item your way. Sometimes it works in your favour.

It's important that we all work together to make these programs happen. It's unfortunate that there's a need for our programs, but there is. When you operate a meal program, you help solve a serious problem in your community. For some people, you make all the difference in the world!

Appendix A

A Sample Five-Week Menu Plan

The following menus are suggestions for an elementary school sit-down daily breakfast program with a five-week menu rotation. It's also suitable for a program that caters to seniors.

If you wish to adapt this menu for older students or non-senior adults, you'll need to increase the portions.

The recipes and portions for these menus are in Appendix B—Recipes and Serving Suggestions.

WEEK 1	Monday	Tuesday	Wednesday	Thursday	Friday
Main	Toast	Yogurt and granola	Ham-and-cheese melt	Carrot-spice muffin	Cereal
Alternate	Cereal	Blueberry-crumble muffin	Cereal	Yogurt and granola	Carrot-spice muffin
Gluten-free	Toast	Yogurt and granola	Ham-and-cheese melt	Yogurt and granola	Cereal
Fruit/vegetable	Apple slices	Fruit salad	Cucumber slices	Orange slices	Banana half
Beverage(s)	Milk and water	Milk and water	Juice and water	Milk and water	Water

WEEK 2	Monday	Tuesday	Wednesday	Thursday	Friday
Main	Toast	Bacon-cheddar muffin	Granola bar	Blueberry pancakes	Banana bake
Alternate	Yogurt and granola	Cereal	Bacon-cheddar muffin	Yogurt and granola	Cereal
Gluten-free	Toast	Cereal	Yogurt and granola	Blueberry pancakes	Cereal
Fruit/vegetable	Orange slices	Carrot sticks	Shrek smoothie	Fruit salad	Apple slices
Beverage(s)	Milk and water	Juice and water	Water	Milk and water	Milk, juice, and water

WEEK 3	Monday	Tuesday	Wednesday	Thursday	Friday
Main	Cereal	Ham-and-cheese quesadilla	Strawberry-swirl muffin	Toast	Loaded carrot bake
Alternate	Yogurt and granola	Yogurt and granola	Cereal	Yogurt and granola	Yogurt and granola
Gluten-free	Yogurt and granola	Ham-and-cheese melt	Cereal	Toast	Yogurt and granola
Fruit/vegetable	Banana half	Sweet pepper strips	Peach slices	Cherry tomatoes	Grapes
Beverage(s)	Water	Milk and water	Milk and water	Juice	Milk and water

WEEK 4	Monday	Tuesday	Wednesday	Thursday	Friday
Main	Yogurt and granola	Toast	Loaded chocolate bake	Granola bar	Fruit loaf
Alternate	Cereal	Yogurt and granola	Cereal	Strawberry-swirl muffin	Yogurt and granola
Gluten-free	Yogurt and granola	Toast	Cereal	Cereal	Yogurt and granola
Fruit/vegetable	Fruit salad	Apple slices	Carrot sticks	Shrek smoothie	Orange slices
Beverage(s)	Juice and water	Milk and water	Milk and water	Water	Milk and water

WEEK 5	Monday	Tuesday	Wednesday	Thursday	Friday
Main	Cereal	Blueberry-crumble muffin	Breakfast bread	Toast	Pumpkin-spice pancakes
Alternate	Yogurt and granola	Yogurt and granola	Cereal	Yogurt and granola	Cereal
Gluten-free	Cereal	Yogurt and granola	Cereal	Toast	Pumpkin-spice pancakes
Fruit/vegetable	Half a banana	Raisins	Celery sticks	Melon sticks	Fruit salad
Beverage(s)	Water	Milk and water	Milk, juice, and water	Milk and water	Milk, juice, and water

Appendix B

Recipes and Serving Suggestions

The following recipes are portioned for elementary school kids. They're also suitable for programs that cater to seniors.

If you're running a program for older kids or non-senior adults, you'll need to increase the portion sizes. High school students, for example, usually eat about twice as much as younger kids.

Apple Slices

Yield: approximately 50 servings
Apple slices should be prepared on the day they're served.

INGREDIENTS

15 mL	lemon juice	1 tbsp
30 mL	water	2 tbsp
11	apples	

DIRECTIONS

1. In a large bowl, combine the lemon juice and water.
2. Core each apple.
3. On a cutting board, cut each apple into quarters lengthwise.
4. Cut each quarter into three slices lengthwise.
5. Toss the apple slices in the lemon juice and water.
6. Serve two or three slices to each person.

Banana Halves

Yield: approximately 50 servings
Banana halves should be prepared just before they're served.

INGREDIENTS

25	bananas

DIRECTIONS
1. On a cutting board, cut each unpeeled banana in half widthwise.
2. Make a lengthwise cut through the peel on each half, about an inch long. This will make the banana half easier to peel.
3. Serve one banana half to each person.
4. If you have leftover bananas, peel them and put them in a freezer bag.
5. Label the bag with the date and the number of whole bananas it contains. Put it in the freezer.

Banana Bake

Yield: approximately 60 servings
This recipe can be prepared a day or two before it's served.

INGREDIENTS

8	eggs	
18	bananas, mashed	
500 mL	unsweetened apple sauce	2 cups
45 mL	vanilla	3 tbsp
500 mL	sugar	2 cups
2,125 mL	flour	8½ cups
20 mL	baking powder	4 tsp

DIRECTIONS

1. Preheat the oven to 175°C (350°F).
2. In a large mixing bowl, beat the eggs.
3. Add in the bananas, apple sauce, and vanilla and mix on medium speed until the mixture is smooth.
4. In another large bowl, combine the sugar, flour, and baking powder.
5. Add the wet ingredients to the dry ingredients. Combine until the mixture is completely wet. Do not overmix.
6. Pour the mixture into a four-inch-deep (10 centimetres) hotel pan sprayed with oil and then lined with parchment paper.
7. Bake at 175°C (350°F) for 45 minutes.
8. Check by sticking a knife or toothpick into the centre of the loaf. If it comes out clean, the loaf is done.

9. If the loaf isn't done, turn the pan so it faces the opposite direction and put it back in the oven for another 20 minutes. (If you're baking two loaves, rotate and switch the pans from top to bottom.)
10. Check the loaf again.
11. If the loaf still isn't done, keep baking and check it every 10 or 15 minutes.
12. Once the loaf is done, remove the pan from the oven and cover with saran wrap, poking holes in it if the loaf is still warm.
13. Place the pan in the refrigerator. Place it atop a couple of towels if the loaf is still warm.
14. Before serving, cut the loaf into 60 pieces, 6 across and 10 down.

Breakfast Bread

Yield: approximately 60 servings
This recipe can be prepared and baked a day or two before it's served.

INGREDIENTS

5	bell peppers, red and green combined (or frozen leftover peppers)	
~1,125 mL	water	~4½ cups
2,375 mL	unsifted whole wheat flour	9½ cups
20 mL	baking powder	4 tbsp
750 mL	diced ham (¼ of a toupie ham, skinned and diced)	3 cups
1,125 mL	grated cheddar cheese	4½ cups
175 mL	oil	¾ cup

DIRECTIONS

1. Preheat the oven to 200°C (400°F).
2. Sauté the peppers.
3. Whiz the cooked peppers in a blender just until they are minced. If necessary, add one or two tablespoons (15 or 30 millilitres) of water from the measured water.
4. Strain over a bowl and let the mixture sit for a few minutes, until the liquid separates from the minced peppers.
5. Strain the mixture, reserving the liquid. Set the pulp aside.
6. Add water to the pepper liquid to make up 4½ cups (1,125 millilitres).
7. Combine the flour and the baking powder.

8. Add the pepper/water solution, three-quarters of the ham, and the oil to the flour mixture. Use gloved hands to mix everything until a dough forms.
9. Turn out the dough onto a floured cutting board. Knead the dough until a ball forms. Do not overwork the dough.
10. Pat or roll out the dough in a four-inch-deep (10 centimetres) hotel pan lined with parchment paper.
11. Score the dough with a knife.
12. Spread the pepper pulp on top of the dough.
13. Bake at 200°C (400°F) for 40 minutes.
14. Insert a knife or toothpick into the centre of the bread. If it comes out clean, the bread is done.
15. If the bread isn't done, turn the pan so it faces the opposite direction and put it back in the oven for another 10 to 15 minutes.
16. Check the loaf again.
17. If the bread still isn't done, keep baking and checking it every 15 minutes. (If you're baking two loaves, rotate and switch the pans from one rack to the other.)
18. Remove from the oven and allow the bread to cool in the pan.
19. Cover the pan with saran wrap, poking holes in it if the breakfast bread is still warm.
20. Place the pan in the refrigerator. Place it atop a couple of towels if the loaf is still warm.
21. Just before serving, arrange the remaining ham and the cheese on top of the bread and place it in a 200°C (400°F) oven until the cheese melts and the bread is warmed through.
22. Cut the bread into 60 pieces, 6 across and 10 down.

Carrot Sticks

Yield: approximately 50 servings
Carrot sticks can be prepared a day or two before they're served and stored in water in the refrigerator.

INGREDIENTS

8	large carrots

DIRECTIONS

1. Wash and peel each carrot. (Unpeeled carrots can transmit dirt and bacteria if they're not cooked.)
2. Cut the ends off each carrot. Discard the ends.
3. On a cutting board, cut each carrot into two or three pieces widthwise, so each piece is about the size of your little finger.
4. Cut each piece in half lengthwise.
5. Slice each piece into strips.
6. Put the carrot sticks in a container.
7. Cover and label the container. Keep it in the refrigerator until you're ready to serve the carrot sticks.
8. Give each person three or more carrot sticks.

Celery Sticks

Yield: approximately 50 servings

Celery sticks can be prepared a day or two before they're served and stored in water in the refrigerator.

INGREDIENTS

1	celery bunch

DIRECTIONS

1. On a cutting board, cut the ends off the celery bunch. This will separate the stalks. Discard the ends.
2. Wash the stalks.
3. Clean the cutting board, if necessary.
4. On the cutting board, cut each celery stalk into 2½-inch (6-centimetre) pieces, the size of your pinky. You should get two or three pieces from each stalk.
5. Cut each piece lengthwise into two or three pieces.
6. Put the celery sticks in a container.
7. Cover and label the container. Keep it in the refrigerator until you're ready to serve the celery sticks.
8. Give each person three or more celery sticks.

Cereal

Yield: approximately 60 servings

Dry cereal will last for some time in a sealed container, depending on its expiry date.

INGREDIENTS

3 (700-gram/ 25-ounce)	boxes of ready-to-serve cereal, assorted
	milk

DIRECTIONS

1. Allow each person to choose a cereal.
2. Pour the cereal into a bowl.
3. Pour milk over the cereal.
4. Keep any unused cereal in a sealed container. Don't mix new and old cereal. Instead, be sure the container is washed and dried before refilling it.

Gluten-Free Option

Provide one type of gluten-free cereal in addition to the three regular types.

Cherry Tomatoes

Yield: approximately 50 servings
Cherry tomatoes can be prepared a day or two before they're served.

INGREDIENTS

3 (350-gram/ 12-ounce)	baskets of cherry tomatoes	approximately 150 tomatoes

DIRECTIONS

1. Wash the tomatoes.
2. Remove and discard the stems.
3. Put the tomatoes in a container.
4. Cover and label the container. Keep it in the refrigerator until you're ready to serve the tomatoes.
5. Give each person three or more tomatoes.

Cucumber Slices

Yield: approximately 60 servings
Cucumber slices should be prepared the same day they're served.

INGREDIENTS

2	long English cucumbers

DIRECTIONS

1. Wash the cucumbers.
2. If your clients are elderly and may have digestive problems, peel the cucumbers.
3. On a cutting board, cut the ends off the cucumbers. Discard the ends.
4. Cut each cucumber into thin slices widthwise, so they look like coins.
5. Put the cucumber slices in a container.
6. Cover and label the container. Keep it in the refrigerator until you're ready to serve the cucumber slices.
7. Give each person three or more cucumber slices.

Fruit Loaf with Variations

Yield: approximately 60 servings

This recipe can be prepared and baked the day before it's served.

This is a basic recipe that you can change to yield several variations. Instructions for the variations follow the directions.

INGREDIENTS

3,000 mL	flour	12⅔ cups
750 mL	sugar	3 cups
40 mL	baking powder	2 tbsp plus 2 tsp
500 mL	margarine or butter	2 cups
16	eggs	
175 mL	juice (see Variations, below)	¾ cup
1,060 mL	milk	4¼ cups
500 to 1,000 mL	fruit, dried or fresh (see Variations, below)	2 to 4 cups

DIRECTIONS

1. Preheat the oven to 175°C (350°F).
2. In a large bowl, combine the flour, sugar, and baking powder.
3. In another bowl, cream the margarine. Gradually add the eggs until the mixture is smooth.
4. Beat the milk and the juice into the wet mixture.
5. Add the wet mixture to the dry ingredients. Mix thoroughly.
6. Fold in the fruit.
7. Pour the mixture into a hotel pan sprayed with oil and then lined with parchment paper.

8. Bake at 175°C (350°F) for 50 minutes.
9. Insert a knife or toothpick into the centre of the loaf. If it comes out clean, the loaf is done.
10. If the loaf isn't done, turn the pan so it faces the opposite direction and put it back in the oven for another 10 to 15 minutes. (If you're baking two loaves, rotate and switch the pans from one rack to the other.)
11. Check the loaf again. Be sure the temperature in the centre of the loaf reaches 65°C (150°F).
12. Remove the loaf from the oven and allow it to cool in the pan.
13. Cover the pan with saran wrap, poking holes in it if the loaf is still warm.
14. Place the pan in the refrigerator. Place it atop a couple of towels if the loaf is still warm.
15. Just before serving, remove the loaf from the refrigerator and slice it.

Variations

Lemon-Cranberry Loaf
1. Use lemon juice instead of fruit juice.
2. Use 500 mL (2 cups) of cranberries.
3. After the loaf is baked:
4. Mix 45 mL (3 tbsp) of lemon juice with 250 mL (1 cup) of icing sugar.
5. Drizzle it on top of the loaf.
6. Allow the loaf to cool normally.

Lemon-Blueberry Loaf
1. Use orange juice instead of fruit juice.
2. Use 750 mL (3 cups) of blueberries.

Peach-Spice Loaf
1. Add the following to the dry ingredients:

- 45 mL (3 tbsp) cinnamon
- 5 mL (1 tsp) cloves
- 5 mL (1 tsp) allspice

2. Use two 796 mL (27-ounce) cans of peaches:
   a. Use the juice to help make up the 175 mL (¾ cup) of juice and add water to make up for the rest of the measurement.
   b. Dice the peaches into small pieces.

Cinnamon-Swirl Loaf

1. Use any kind of fruit juice.
2. Combine 45 mL (3 tbsp) of cinnamon and 250 mL (1 cup) of brown sugar with 125 mL (½ cup) of oil.
3. Pour half of the batter into the hotel pan.
4. Top the whole surface with half of the cinnamon-and-sugar mix.
5. Pour in the rest of the batter.
6. Top it with the rest of the cinnamon-and-sugar mix.
7. Place a serving knife upright to the bottom of the batter and swirl it thoroughly around in the pan.

Fruit Salad

Yield: approximately 50 or 60 servings

Fruit salad should be prepared the same day it's served. (Canned fruit can be kept in the unopened can in the refrigerator for a day or two prior to serving so it can be served chilled.)

INGREDIENTS

3 kg can	fruit salad	106 ounces

DIRECTIONS

1. Open the can and strain the juice into a large container.
2. Put the juice in the refrigerator for later use in smoothies, mixed juices, and baked goods.
3. Use a 60 mL (¼ cup) measure to portion out the fruit salad.
4. If you have fruit salad left over, spread it on a baking sheet covered with parchment paper. Cover it with saran wrap and place it in the freezer.
5. Once the fruit is frozen, place it in a ziplock bag for later use in fruit smoothies.

Granola

Yield: approximately 96 servings

This recipe can be prepared and baked the day before it's served. It will keep in a ziplock bag in the refrigerator for a month.

Be sure to use quick-cooking rolled oats that are labelled "gluten-free." Although oats naturally contain no gluten, they're often contaminated by gluten in processing facilities.

INGREDIENTS

250 mL	liquid honey	1 cup
125 mL	olive oil	½ cup
30 mL	vanilla	2 tbsp
3,000 mL	gluten-free quick-cooking rolled oats	12 cups
45 mL	cinnamon	3 tbsp
125 mL	brown or golden-yellow sugar	½ cup

DIRECTIONS

1. Preheat the oven to 200°C (400°F).
2. In a large bowl, combine the honey, oil, and vanilla.
3. Add the oats, cinnamon, and brown sugar to the liquid mixture.
4. Use your gloved hands to thoroughly mix all of the ingredients together.
5. Spread the granola mixture on two baking sheets lined with parchment paper.
6. Bake at 200°C (400°F) for 15 minutes.
7. Stir and flip the granola.

8. Bake for another 15 minutes and flip the granola again. Do this until the granola is golden-brown throughout.

9. Serve by spooning 15 or 30 mL (1 or 2 tbsp) of granola over a serving of yogurt.

10. Place any leftover granola in an airtight container or a ziplock bag and label it with the date. Freeze it for future use.

Granola Bars

Yield: approximately 60 servings

Granola bars will last for several weeks (depending on their expiry date) in a sealed container.

INGREDIENTS

2 large boxes	commercial granola bars	approximately 96 bars

DIRECTIONS

1. Give each person a granola bar. If there are different flavours, allow each person to choose one.
2. If you have leftover granola bars, store them in a cupboard, sealed and/or in their original box.

Grapes

Yield: approximately 60 servings
Grapes can be prepared a day or two before they're served.

INGREDIENTS

3 large bunches	grapes

DIRECTIONS

1. Wash the grapes.
2. Use kitchen scissors to cut the stems into bunches of five to seven grapes.
3. Put the grapes in a container.
4. Cover and label the container. Keep it in the refrigerator until you're ready to serve the grapes.
5. Give each person one bunch of grapes.

Ham-and-Cheese Melts with Variations

Yield: approximately 60 servings
This recipe can be prepared the day before it's baked and served.

INGREDIENTS

½	toupie ham, quartered, skinned, and thinly sliced	
40	buns, sliced in half (see Variations, below)	
1,000 mL	grated cheddar cheese	4 cups

DIRECTIONS
1. Place the buns face up in a hotel pan lined with parchment paper.
2. Place one slice of ham on each bun.
3. Top the ham with 1 slice or 15 mL (1 tbsp) of grated cheese.
4. Place another piece of parchment paper on top of the buns.
5. Place a second layer of buns, ham, and cheese atop the first. Keep doing this until you run out of buns.
6. Cover the pan with a final layer of parchment paper and refrigerate.
7. The next day, preheat the oven to 200°C (400°F).
8. Carefully lift out one layer of parchment paper and buns and place it on a baking sheet.
9. Bake at 200°C (400°F) until the cheese melts. This should take just a couple of minutes. Repeat until all the ham-and-cheese melts are baked.
10. If you're not serving these right away, carefully lift the parchment paper and buns off of the baking sheet and layer them back into the hotel pan with parchment paper between each layer.

11. Serve the ham-and-cheese melts while they're warm.

Variations

Gluten-Free Ham-and-Cheese Melts

1.   Use gluten-free buns or bread.

Ham-and-Cheese Quesadillas

Yield: approximately 50 servings
This recipe can be prepared the day before it's baked and served.

INGREDIENTS

36	whole-wheat tortillas	
750 mL	small-diced ham (¼ toupie ham, skinned and diced)	3 cups
2,125 mL	grated cheddar cheese	8½ cups
	salsa (optional)	
	guacamole (optional)	
	sour cream (optional)	

DIRECTIONS

1. Lay half of the tortillas side by side in a hotel pan lined with parchment paper.
2. Sprinkle each tortilla with ham and cheese, and cover with another tortilla.
3. Place another piece of parchment paper on top of the quesadillas.
4. Place a second layer of tortillas, ham, and cheese atop the first. Keep doing this until you run out of tortillas.
5. Cover the pan with a final layer of parchment paper and refrigerate.
6. The next day, preheat the oven to 65°C (150°F).
7. Heat two nonstick pans over medium heat.
8. Cook each quesadilla until it's golden-brown on the bottom and the cheese is melted. Flip and cook the quesadilla for a little longer.

9. On a cutting board, cut each quesadilla in half and then cut each half into three pieces.

10. Place the cut pieces in a hotel pan lined with parchment paper.

11. Place the pan in the oven and turn it off. The residual heat will keep the quesadillas warm until you serve them.

12. Give each person two or three pieces.

13. If your clients are young children, you can serve the quesadillas plain. If your clients are adults, depending on your budget, you may want to make half a quesadilla per person and offer salsa, guacamole, and sour cream when the client comes down the line. You making the portion size is much better than leaving it up to the client.

Loaded Carrot Bake

Yield: approximately 45 servings

This recipe can be prepared and baked the day before it's served.

If you'd like to make muffin-style single servings, you can bake the batter in muffin tins instead of a hotel pan.

INGREDIENTS

1,125 mL	flour	4½ cups
375 mL	sugar	1½ cups
15 mL	baking powder	1 tbsp
30 mL	cinnamon	2 tbsp
6	eggs	
560 mL	olive oil	2¼ cups
15 mL	vanilla	1 tbsp
3	bananas, mashed	
750 mL	crushed pineapple	3 cups
1,125 mL	grated carrots	4½ cups

WIPPED TOPPING

1,125 mL	whipping cream	4¼ cups
45 mL	vanilla	3 tbsp

DIRECTIONS

1. Preheat the oven to 175°C (350°F).
2. In a large bowl, whisk together the flour, sugar, baking powder, and cinnamon.

3. In another bowl, whisk together the eggs, olive oil, and vanilla.
4. Add the mashed bananas and pineapple to the wet ingredients.
5. Combine the wet and dry ingredients.
6. Mix in the grated carrots.
7. Pour the mixture into a hotel pan sprayed with oil and then lined with parchment paper.
8. Bake at 175°C (350°F) for 40 minutes.
9. Insert a knife or toothpick into the centre of the bake. If it comes out clean, the bake is done.
10. If the carrot bake isn't done, turn the pan so it faces the opposite direction and put it back in the oven for another 10 to 15 minutes. (If you're making two carrot bakes, rotate and switch the pans from top to bottom.)
11. Check the carrot bake again. Be sure the temperature in the centre reaches 65°C (150°F).
12. Remove the pan from the oven and allow it to cool.
13. Cover the pan with saran wrap, poking holes in it if the carrot bake is still warm.
14. Place the pan in the refrigerator. Place it atop a couple of towels if the carrot bake is still warm.
15. Just before serving, remove the carrot bake from the refrigerator and slice it.
16. Whip the cream. Fold in the vanilla. Do not add sugar.
17. Serve the carrot bake with a dollop of whipped cream on each slice.

Loaded Chocolate Bake

Yield: approximately 45 servings

This recipe can be prepared and baked the day before it's served.

   If you'd like to make muffin-style single servings, you can bake the batter in muffin tins instead of a hotel pan.

INGREDIENTS

1,000 mL	white flour	4 cups
500 mL	whole wheat flour	2 cups
625 mL	sugar	2½ cups
22 mL	baking soda	4½ tsp
250 mL	cocoa (sifted)	1 cup
5 mL	cinnamon	1 tsp
1.25 mL	allspice	¼ tsp
1.25 mL	cloves	¼ tsp
750 mL	puréed pumpkin	3 cups
750 mL	grated zucchini (patted dry after grating)	3 cups
375 mL	olive oil	1½ cups
30 mL	vanilla	2 tbsp

DIRECTIONS

1. Preheat the oven to 175°C (350°F).
2. In a large bowl, combine the white and whole-wheat flour, sugar, baking soda, sifted cocoa, and pumpkin-pie spice.
3. Add the puréed pumpkin, zucchini, oil, and vanilla. Mix well.

4. Pour the mixture into a hotel pan sprayed with oil and then lined with parchment paper.

5. Bake at 175°C (350°F) for 45 minutes.

6. Insert a knife or a toothpick into the centre of the chocolate bake. If it comes out clean, the chocolate bake is done.

7. If the chocolate bake isn't done, turn the pan so it faces the opposite direction and put it back in the oven for another 10 to 15 minutes. (If you're making two chocolate bakes, rotate and switch the pans from top to bottom.)

8. Check the chocolate bake again. Be sure the temperature in the centre reaches 65°C (150°F).

9. Remove the chocolate bake from the oven and allow it to cool in the pan.

10. Cover the pan with saran wrap, poking holes in it if the chocolate bake is still warm.

11. Place the pan in the refrigerator. Place it atop a couple of towels if the chocolate bake is still warm.

12. Just before serving, remove the chocolate bake from the refrigerator and slice it.

Melon Slices

Yield: approximately 60 servings
Melon slices should be prepared the same day they're served.

INGREDIENTS

2	melons, any type (cantaloupe, honeydew, muskmelon, etc.)

Or

1	watermelon

DIRECTIONS

1. Wash the melons.
2. On a cutting board, cut each melon in half widthwise.
3. Use a large spoon to remove the seeds and clean the centre of the melon. You can skip this step if you're using a watermelon.
4. Place each half-melon cut-side down on a cutting board. Use a sharp knife to remove the skin, working from the top to the bottom of the melon half.
5. Cut each peeled half lengthwise into four pieces.
6. Slice each piece widthwise into 10 slices.
7. Put the melon slices in a container.
8. Cover and label the container. Keep it in the refrigerator until you're ready to serve the melon slices.
9. Give each person one or two melon slices.

Muffins with Variations

Yield: approximately 96 servings
This recipe can be prepared and baked the day before it's served.

This is a basic recipe that you can change to yield several variations. Instructions for the variations follow the directions.

Note: The Fruit Loaf with Variations recipe also works as a muffin recipe and will save you the cost of purchasing bags of muffin mix. However, muffin mix will save you time if you are short-handed.

INGREDIENTS

5 (900-gram/ 32-ounce)	bags of commercial muffin mix
	other ingredients called for in the package directions (see Variations, below)

DIRECTIONS

1. Preheat the oven to 200°C (400°F).
2. In a large bowl, combine the 5 bags of commercial muffin mix.
3. Follow the package directions to mix the batter.
4. Following the variations, below, add the ingredients for the type of muffin you're making.
5. Fill muffin tins sprayed with oil.
6. Bake at 200°C (400°F) for the time prescribed in the package directions.
7. Remove the muffins from the tins and allow them to cool on racks.
8. Layer the cooled muffins in a four-inch-deep (10 centimetres) hotel pan lined with parchment paper, placing parchment paper between the layers.

9. Cover the pan with saran wrap, poking holes in it if the muffins are still warm.
10. Place the pan in the refrigerator. Place it atop a couple of towels if the loaf is still warm.

Variations

Bacon-Cheddar Muffins
1. Add the following to the batter:
   - 2 packages of bacon, cooked and diced
   - 500 mL (2 cups) of grated cheddar

Strawberry-Swirl Muffins
1. Once the batter is in the muffin tin, add 5 mL (1 tsp) of strawberry jam to each muffin.
2. Use a knife to swirl the jam around in each muffin cup.

Blueberry-Crumble Muffins
1. Add 500 mL (2 cups) of blueberries to the batter.
2. Top each muffin with leftover granola.

Carrot-Spice Muffins
1. Add the following to the dry ingredients:
   - 90 mL (6 tbsp) cinnamon
   - 5 mL (1 tsp) nutmeg
   - 5 mL (1 tsp) allspice
2. Add 750 mL (3 cups) of grated carrots to the batter.

Orange Slices

Yield: approximately 60 servings
Orange slices should be prepared the same day they're served.

INGREDIENTS

12	navel oranges (or other firm-skinned oranges)

DIRECTIONS

1. Wash the oranges.
2. On a cutting board, cut the ends off each orange. Discard the ends.
3. Cut each orange in half lengthwise.
4. Lay each orange half cut side down. Slice the orange into five pieces, lengthwise or widthwise.
5. Put the orange slices in a container.
6. Cover and label the container. Keep it in the refrigerator until you're ready to serve the orange slices.
7. Give each person two orange slices.

Pancakes with Variations

Yield: approximately 60 servings
This recipe can be prepared and cooked the day before it's served.

INGREDIENTS

2,500 mL	flour	10 cups
250 mL	sugar	1 cup
70 mL	baking powder	⅓ cup
8	eggs	
750 mL	unsweetened apple sauce	3 cups
2,000 mL	milk	8 cups
45 mL	vanilla	3 tbsp
125 mL	margarine or butter, melted	½ cup
	syrup	

DIRECTIONS

1. Preheat the griddle to 120°C (250°F). Place a frying pan on each element and set it to medium-low.
2. Preheat the oven to 65°C (150°F).
3. In a large bowl, thoroughly combine the flour, sugar, and baking powder.
4. In another large bowl, beat together the eggs, apple sauce, milk, vanilla, and melted margarine or butter.
5. Add the wet ingredients to the dry ingredients. Mix until the batter is smooth. Do not overmix.

6. Use a 60 mL (¼ cup) measure to measure pancake batter into the hot frying pans. Try not to let the pancakes touch.
7. When the pancakes start to bubble, use a food turner (also known as a plastic spatula or a pancake flipper) to turn them over.
8. Cook the pancakes for a few minutes more.
9. Place the cooked pancakes in a hotel pan lined with parchment paper. Layer them, with parchment paper separating the layers. Place another piece of parchment paper on the top layer.
10. Cool and place the pancakes in the refrigerator.
11. The next day, preheat the oven to 200°C (400°F).
12. For preteen kids, cut the pancakes into bite-sized pieces and put them back in the parchment-lined hotel pan. For older kids or adults, keep the pancakes whole.
13. When the pancakes are warm, give each person one large spoonful or one or two pancakes. Allow them to add the syrup themselves.

Variations

Gluten-Free Pancakes
1. Use a gluten-free pancake mix.
2. Make the pancakes to order for anyone following a gluten-free diet.

Pumpkin-Spice Pancakes
1. Add the following to the dry ingredients:
    * 20 mL (4 tsp) cinnamon
    * 10 mL (2 tsp) nutmeg
    * 5 mL (1 tsp) cloves
2. Use pumpkin purée instead of apple sauce.

Blueberry Pancakes
1. Stir in 750 mL (3 cups) of fresh or thawed blueberries just before you pour the batter into the frying pans.

2.   If you prefer, you can stir in frozen blueberries about 20 minutes before cooking. This will give the blueberries time to thaw, so the pancakes will cook faster.

Peach Slices

Yield: approximately 60 servings
Peach slices should be prepared the same day they're served.

INGREDIENTS

3 kg can	peach slices	106 ounces

DIRECTIONS
1. Open the can.
2. Pour the contents of the can into a large bowl.
3. Use a slotted spoon to serve the peach slices. Give each person one spoonful.
4. If you have peaches left over, drain and spread them on a baking sheet lined with parchment paper. Cover them with saran wrap and place the sheet in the freezer.
5. Once the peaches are frozen, place them in a ziplock bag for later use in fruit smoothies.
6. Put the juice in the refrigerator for later use in smoothies, mixed juices, and baked goods.

Raisins

Yield: approximately 60 servings
Raisins will last for some time in a sealed container, depending on their expiry date. Label the container with the expiry date from the original bag.

INGREDIENTS

large bag	raisins

DIRECTIONS
1. Open the bag.
2. Use a tablespoon to give each person a few raisins.
3. Seal the bag and place it in a dry storage area.

Shrek Smoothie

Yield: approximately 45 servings
Smoothies should be prepared just before they're served.

INGREDIENTS

750 mL	packed sliced kale, fresh or frozen	3 cups
125 mL	water	½ cup
750 mL	frozen whole strawberries	1.65 lbs
750 mL	frozen bananas or other fruit	1.65 lbs
45 mL	honey	3 tbsp
45 mL	vanilla	3 tbsp
2,000 mL	full-fat milk	8 cups
2,000 mL	water	8 cups

DIRECTIONS

1. Whiz the kale with the water in a full-size household blender until it's nearly liquified. Pour it into a bowl and set it aside.
2. Place 250 mL (1 cup) of frozen strawberries, 250 mL (1 cup) of frozen bananas or other fruit, 250 mL (1 cup) of the blended kale, 15 mL (1 tbsp) of honey, and 15 mL (1 tbsp) of vanilla in the blender.
3. Add milk and water (in equal portions) to fill the blender.
4. Blend until the mixture is smooth.
5. Pour the smoothie into a juice jug. It may separate if it sits too long, so keep a large spoon on hand to stir the smoothie.
6. Repeat the recipe two more times.
7. Pour into small glasses and serve.

Sweet Pepper Strips

Yield: approximately 60 servings
Pepper slices should be prepared the same day they're served.

INGREDIENTS

3	red peppers
3	green peppers

DIRECTIONS

1. Wash the peppers.
2. Cut the ends off each pepper, leaving the core intact.
3. Cut the pepper in half lengthwise.
4. Remove and discard the core from each pepper half.
5. Cut each pepper half into five strips.
6. Put the pepper strips in a container.
7. Cover and label the container. Keep it in the refrigerator until you're ready to serve the pepper strips.
8. Give each person three pepper strips.
9. Dice and freeze any leftover pepper strips for later use in a breakfast bread.

Toast with Gluten-Free Variation

Yield: approximately 50 servings
Toast should be made right before it's served.

INGREDIENTS

	honey
	jam
	cream cheese
5 loaves	bread (see Gluten-Free Variation, below)
	margarine

DIRECTIONS

1. Turn on the toaster. Keep it going throughout breakfast.
2. If your clients are high school kids or adults, place the honey, jam, and cream cheese where they can help themselves.
3. Place several slices of bread in the toaster intake.
4. Continuously add bread to the toaster so there are always two or three slices in progress.
5. Once the bread is toasted, spread each slice with a thin layer of margarine.
6. Place the toast in a hotel pan and cover it to keep it warm. It will keep for about 30 minutes before it starts to get soft.
7. Give each person one piece of toast.
8. If your clients are elementary school children or seniors, offer them a dollop of honey, jam, or cream cheese as you serve the toast. Some seniors may need help with spreading.

Gluten-Free Variation

1. Use gluten-free bread for a child who can't eat regular bread. If the bread is frozen, you'll probably have to put it through the toaster twice.

2. Make the gluten-free toast to order as the person arrives.

Yogurt and Granola

Yield: approximately 60 servings
Yogurt will keep in the refrigerator for several weeks, depending on its expiry date. Granola will keep in a sealed container for a month.

INGREDIENTS

2,000 mL	yogurt (any flavour; vanilla is good)	8 cups
3,000 mL	granola (see recipe for Granola, above)	12 cups

DIRECTIONS
1. Remove one container from the refrigerator. Keep the others refrigerated until you need them.
2. Place a large spoonful of yogurt in a bowl for each person.
3. Offer each person a spoonful of granola on top of the yogurt.

Appendix C

Production Sheets for a Five-Week Menu Plan

Before the First Five-Week Menu Cycle Begins

Notice that the production sheet for Monday of Week 1 asks you to move a bag of granola from the freezer to the refrigerator, while the production sheet for Tuesday of Week 1 instructs you to move a bag of blueberry-crumble muffins from the freezer to the refrigerator. At least a day or two before you launch Week 1 of your first menu cycle, therefore, you'll need to make the granola and the blueberry-crumble muffins before your program launches.

Once the program is underway, you'll already have the granola and muffins in the freezer when Week 1 rolls around again. The instructions to mix and bake them appear on later production sheets.

Friday Before Week 1

Set-Up

o   Move six loaves of bread (including one gluten-free loaf) from the freezer to the refrigerator for Monday's breakfast.

o   Make a batch of granola for Tuesday's breakfast.

o   Mix and bake four dozen blueberry-crumble muffins for Tuesday's breakfast.

Week 1

MONDAY

Set-Up

o   Sign in.

o   Turn on washing machine.

o   Put out the tables and chairs.

o   Put out the plates, bowls, glasses, coffee cups (if you're serving coffee), knives, spoons, and napkins.

o   If you're serving adults, turn the coffee maker on and put out milk and sugar for the coffee.

o   Put away the clean dishes.

o   Fold and put away the clean laundry.

o   Put out the milk and drinking water.

o   If you're using coffee carafes, fill and put them out.

o   Wash, slice, and put out the apples.

o   Put out the honey, jam, and cream cheese for the toast.

o   Plug in and turn on the toaster. Start making toast (today's main and gluten-free menu choices) as soon as the toaster is hot. Keep a few slices of gluten-free bread available for those who need it.

o   Put out two kinds of cereal (today's alternate menu choice) and milk.

o   Move a bag of granola from the freezer to the refrigerator for Tuesday's breakfast.

o   Put an unopened can of fruit salad in the refrigerator for Tuesday's breakfast.
o   Slice, peel, and dice the ham for Wednesday's breakfast (ham-and-cheese melts). Store it in a sealed container in the refrigerator.
o   Remove the buns for Wednesday's breakfast from the freezer. Store them on the counter.

Clean-Up

o   Use disinfectant spray and a clean cloth to wipe down the tables.
o   Put away the tables and chairs.
o   Empty, clean, and refill the coffee machine.
o   Count the used dishes and record the number of meals served on the client log sheet.
o   Fill and turn on the dishwasher.
o   Use a cloth to wash all of the sinks with soap and water, rinsing them clean.
o   Use disinfectant spray and a clean cloth to wipe down the countertops.
o   Make sure all of the appliances are unplugged and that the oven and stove elements are turned off.
o   Put all of the used towels and cloths into the washing machine.
o   Move laundry to dryer and turn it on.
o   Sign out. Thank you!

TUESDAY

Set-Up

o   Sign in.
o   Turn on washing machine
o   Put out the tables and chairs.
o   Put out the bowls, glasses, coffee cups (if you're serving coffee), spoons, and napkins.
o   If you're serving adults, turn the coffee maker on and put out milk and sugar for the coffee.

○ Put away the clean dishes.

○ Fold and put away the clean laundry.

○ Preheat the oven to 200°C (400°F).

○ Put out the milk and drinking water.

○ If you're using coffee carafes, fill and put them out.

○ Open the refrigerated can of fruit salad. Portion the fruit salad into serving bowls and put them out.

○ Put out the yogurt and granola (today's main and gluten-free menu choices).

○ Move a bag of blueberry-crumble muffins (today's alternate menu choice) from the freezer to the refrigerator. When someone asks for a muffin, microwave it for about thirty seconds before serving it.

○ Prepare the ham-and-cheese melts for Wednesday's breakfast. Be sure to separate and label those made with gluten-free buns. Cover and place them in the refrigerator.

○ Mix and bake four dozen carrot-spice muffins for Thursday's breakfast. Cool, cover, and place them in the refrigerator.

○ Check granola; if it is low, make another batch on Wednesday.

Clean-Up

○ Use disinfectant spray and a clean cloth to wipe down the tables.

○ Put away the tables and chairs.

○ Empty, clean, and refill the coffee machine.

○ Count the used dishes and record the number of meals served on the client log sheet.

○ Fill and turn on the dishwasher.

○ Use a cloth to wash all of the sinks with soap and water, rinsing them clean.

○ Use disinfectant spray and a clean cloth to wipe down the countertops.

○ Make sure all of the appliances are unplugged and that the oven and stove elements are turned off.

○ Put all of the used towels and cloths into the washing machine.

o Move laundry to dryer and turn it on.
o Sign out. Thank you!

WEDNESDAY

Set-Up
o Sign in.
o Turn on washing machine.
o Put out the tables and chairs.
o Put out the plates, bowls, glasses, coffee cups (if you're serving coffee), knives, forks, spoons, and napkins.
o If you're serving adults, turn the coffee maker on and put out milk and sugar for the coffee.
o Put away the clean dishes.
o Fold and put away the clean laundry.
o Preheat the oven to 200°C (400°F).
o Put out the juice and drinking water.
o If you're using coffee carafes, fill and put them out.
o Wash, peel (if necessary), slice, and put out the cucumbers.
o Put out two kinds of cereal (today's alternate menu choice) and milk.
o Bake and serve the ham-and-cheese melts you prepared on Tuesday (today's main and gluten-free menu choices). Serve them immediately. Keep two or three made with gluten-free buns ready for those who need them.
o Move a bag of granola from the freezer to the refrigerator for Thursday's breakfast. If the granola is getting low, make another batch.

Clean-Up
o Use disinfectant spray and a clean cloth to wipe down the tables.
o Put away the tables and chairs.
o Empty, clean, and refill the coffee machine.
o Count the used dishes and record the number of meals served on the client log sheet.

o   Fill and turn on the dishwasher.

o   Use a cloth to wash all of the sinks with soap and water, rinsing them clean.

o   Use disinfectant spray and a clean cloth to wipe down the countertops.

o   Make sure all of the appliances are unplugged and that the oven and stove elements are turned off.

o   Put all of the used towels and cloths into the washing machine.

o   Move laundry to dryer and turn it on.

o   Sign out. Thank you!

THURSDAY

Set-Up

o   Sign in.

o   Turn on washing machine.

o   Put out the tables and chairs.

o   Put out the plates, bowls, glasses, coffee cups (if you're serving coffee), spoons, and napkins.

o   If you're serving adults, turn the coffee maker on and put out milk and sugar for the coffee.

o   Put away the clean dishes.

o   Fold and put away the clean laundry.

o   Preheat the oven to 200°C (400°F).

o   Put out the milk and drinking water.

o   If you're using coffee carafes, fill and put them out.

o   Wash, slice, and put out the oranges.

o   Put out the yogurt and granola (today's alternate and gluten-free menu choices).

o   Heat the carrot-spice muffins you baked on Tuesday (today's main menu choice) on the top shelf of the oven. Serve them immediately.

o   Put a labelled and dated ziplock bag of carrot-spice muffins in the refrigerator for Friday's breakfast.

o   Place any remaining carrot-spice muffins in a hotel pan in the freezer, so they can freeze individually.

Clean-Up

o   Use disinfectant spray and a clean cloth to wipe down the tables.
o   Put away the tables and chairs.
o   Empty, clean, and refill the coffee machine.
o   Count the used dishes and record the number of meals served on the client log sheet.
o   Fill and turn on the dishwasher.
o   Use a cloth to wash all of the sinks with soap and water, rinsing them clean.
o   Use disinfectant spray and a clean cloth to wipe down the countertops.
o   Make sure all of the appliances are unplugged and that the oven and stove elements are turned off.
o   Put all of the used towels and cloths into the washing machine.
o   Move laundry to dryer and turn it on.
o   Sign out. Thank you!

FRIDAY

Set-Up

o   Sign in.
o   Turn on washing machine.
o   Put out the tables and chairs.
o   Put out the plates, bowls, glasses, coffee cups (if you're serving coffee), spoons, and napkins.
o   If you're serving adults, turn the coffee maker on and put out milk and sugar for the coffee.
o   Put away the clean dishes.
o   Fold and put away the clean laundry.
o   Put out the drinking water.
o   If you're using coffee carafes, fill and put them out.

- Wash, halve, and put out the bananas.
- Put out two types of cereal—one regular and one gluten-free (today's main and gluten-free menu choices; Cheerios and Rice Krispies are gluten-free)—and milk.
- Remove the bag of carrot-spice muffins (today's alternate menu choice) from the refrigerator. When someone asks for a muffin, heat it in the microwave for fifteen seconds.
- Move six loaves of bread (including a gluten-free loaf) from the freezer to the back counter for Monday's breakfast.
- Dice and cook two packages of frozen bacon for use in Tuesday's bacon-cheddar muffins. (Bacon is easier to dice when it's frozen.) When it's cool, put the cooked bacon in a labelled and dated ziplock bag and place it in the freezer.
- Move a bag of granola from the freezer to the refrigerator for Monday's breakfast. If the granola is getting low, make another batch.
- Move Thursday's frozen carrot-spice muffins from the hotel pan into labelled and dated ziplock bags. Place them back in the freezer.
- If any carrot-spice muffins are left over from today's breakfast, put them in a labelled and dated ziplock bag and place it in the freezer.

Clean-Up

- Use disinfectant spray and a clean cloth to wipe down the tables.
- Put away the tables and chairs.
- Empty, clean, and refill the coffee machine.
- Count the used dishes and record the number of meals served on the client log sheet.
- Fill and turn on the dishwasher.
- Use a cloth to wash all of the sinks with soap and water, rinsing them clean.
- Use disinfectant spray and a clean cloth to wipe down the countertops.

- o Make sure all of the appliances are unplugged and that the oven and stove elements are turned off.
- o Put all of the used towels and cloths into the washing machine.
- o Move laundry to dryer and turn it on.
- o Sign out. Thank you!

Week 2

MONDAY

Set-Up
- o Sign in.
- o Turn on washing machine.
- o Put out the tables and chairs.
- o Put out the plates, bowls, glasses, coffee cups (if you're serving coffee), knives, spoons, and napkins.
- o If you're serving adults, turn the coffee maker on and put out milk and sugar for the coffee.
- o Put away the clean dishes.
- o Fold and put away the clean laundry.
- o Turn oven on to 200°C (400°F).
- o Plug in and turn on the toaster. Start making toast (today's main and gluten-free menu choices) as soon as the toaster is hot. Keep a few slices of gluten-free bread available for those who need it.
- o Put out the milk and drinking water.
- o If you're using coffee carafes, fill and put them out.
- o Wash, slice, and put out the oranges.
- o Put out the honey, jam, and cream cheese for the toast.
- o Put out the yogurt and granola (today's alternate menu choice).
- o Mix and bake four dozen bacon-cheddar muffins for Tuesday's breakfast. Cool, cover, and place them in the refrigerator.
- o Peel eighteen bananas. Store them in a covered bowl in the refrigerator. You'll use them on Tuesday to mix the batter for a banana bake.

Clean-Up

o   Use disinfectant spray and a clean cloth to wipe down the tables.

o   Put away the tables and chairs.

o   Empty, clean, and refill the coffee machine.

o   Count the used dishes and record the number of meals served on the client log sheet.

o   Fill and turn on the dishwasher.

o   Use a cloth to wash all of the sinks with soap and water, rinsing them clean.

o   Use disinfectant spray and a clean cloth to wipe down the countertops.

o   Make sure all of the appliances are unplugged and that the oven and stove elements are turned off.

o   Put all of the used towels and cloths into the washing machine.

o   Move laundry to dryer and turn it on.

o   Sign out. Thank you!

TUESDAY

Set-Up

o   Sign in.

o   Turn on washing machine.

o   Put out the tables and chairs.

o   Put out the plates, bowls, glasses, coffee cups (if you're serving coffee), spoons, and napkins.

o   If you're serving adults, turn the coffee maker on and put out milk and sugar for the coffee.

o   Put away the clean dishes.

o   Fold and put away the clean laundry.

o   Preheat the oven to 200°C (400°F).

o   Put out the juice and drinking water.

o   If you're using coffee carafes, fill and put them out.

o   Wash, peel, cut, and put out the carrots.

o   Heat the bacon-cheddar muffins (today's main menu choice) on the top shelf of the oven. Serve them immediately.

o   Put out two types of cereal—one regular and one gluten-free (today's alternate and gluten-free menu choices; Cheerios and Rice Krispies are gluten-free)—and milk.

o   Mix a *plain* batch of pancake batter for Thursday's breakfast. Cover and place the batter in the refrigerator. (You'll add the blueberries just before you cook the pancakes.)

o   Mix the batter for the banana bake for Friday's breakfast. Cover and place the batter in the refrigerator.

o   Put a ziplock bag of bacon-cheddar muffins in the refrigerator for Wednesday's breakfast.

o   Place any remaining bacon-cheddar muffins in a hotel pan in the freezer, so they can freeze individually.

o   Move a bag of granola from the freezer to the refrigerator for Wednesday's breakfast. If the granola is getting low, make another batch.

Clean-Up

o   Use disinfectant spray and a clean cloth to wipe down the tables.

o   Put away the tables and chairs.

o   Empty, clean, and refill the coffee machine.

o   Count the used dishes and record the number of meals served on the client log sheet.

o   Fill and turn on the dishwasher.

o   Use a cloth to wash all of the sinks with soap and water, rinsing them clean.

o   Use disinfectant spray and a clean cloth to wipe down the countertops.

o   Make sure all of the appliances are unplugged and that the oven and stove elements are turned off.

o   Put all of the used towels and cloths into the washing machine.

o   Move laundry to dryer and turn on.

o   Sign out. Thank you!

WEDNESDAY

Set-Up

o   Sign in.

o   Turn on washing machine.

o   Put out the tables and chairs.

o   Put out the plates, bowls, glasses, coffee cups (if you're serving coffee), spoons, and napkins.

o   If you're serving adults, turn the coffee maker on and put out milk and sugar for the coffee.

o   Put away the clean dishes.

o   Fold and put away the clean laundry.

o   Preheat the oven to 175°C (350°F).

o   Put out the drinking water.

o   If you're using coffee carafes, fill and put them out.

o   Prepare and serve the Shrek smoothies.

o   Put out the granola bars (today's main menu choice).

o   Remove the bag of bacon-cheddar muffins (today's alternate menu choice) from the refrigerator. When someone asks for a muffin, heat it in the microwave for fifteen seconds.

o   Put out the yogurt and granola (today's gluten-free menu choice).

o   Move the banana-loaf batter from the refrigerator to the oven and bake it for Friday's breakfast. *Do not* cut the banana bake into pieces today.

o   Add the blueberries to the pancake batter you mixed on Tuesday. Use a griddle and two frying pans to cook the blueberry pancakes. Cover and store them in the refrigerator for Thursday's breakfast.

o   Put an unopened can of fruit salad in the refrigerator for Thursday's breakfast.

o   If any bacon-cheddar muffins are left over from today's breakfast, put them in a labelled and dated ziplock bag and place it in the freezer.

o   Move Tuesday's frozen bacon-cheddar muffins from the hotel pan into labelled and dated ziplock bags. Put them back in the freezer.

o   Move a bag of granola from the freezer to the refrigerator for Thursday's breakfast. If the granola is getting low, make another batch.

Clean-Up

o   Use disinfectant spray and a clean cloth to wipe down the tables.
o   Put away the tables and chairs.
o   Empty, clean, and refill the coffee machine.
o   Count the used dishes and record the number of meals served on the client log sheet.
o   Fill and turn on the dishwasher.
o   Use a cloth to wash all of the sinks with soap and water, rinsing them clean.
o   Use disinfectant spray and a clean cloth to wipe down the countertops.
o   Make sure all of the appliances are unplugged and that the oven and stove elements are turned off.
o   Put all of the used towels and cloths into the washing machine.
o   Move laundry to dryer and turn it on.
o   Sign out. Thank you!

THURSDAY

Set-Up

o   Sign in.
o   Turn on washing machine.
o   Put out the tables and chairs.
o   Put out the plates, bowls, glasses, coffee cups (if you're serving coffee), forks, spoons, and napkins.
o   If you're serving adults, turn the coffee maker on and put out milk and sugar for the coffee.
o   Put away the clean dishes.
o   Fold and put away the clean laundry.

o   Preheat the oven to 200°C (400°F).

o   Put out the milk and drinking water.

o   If you're using coffee carafes, fill and put them out.

o   Open the refrigerated can of fruit salad. Portion the fruit salad into serving bowls and put them out.

o   Put out the syrup for the pancakes.

o   Cut up the blueberry pancakes (today's main and gluten-free menu choices) and heat them on the top shelf of the oven. Serve them immediately. Keep the gluten-free pancake mix and the blueberries available, and make gluten-free pancakes to order for those who need them.

o   Put out the yogurt and granola (today's alternate menu choice).

o   Cut the banana bake you baked on Wednesday into squares, leaving them in place in the pan. Cover and store them in the refrigerator for Friday's breakfast.

o   If the granola is getting low, make sure you have the ingredients to make another batch on Friday.

Clean-Up

o   Use disinfectant spray and a clean cloth to wipe down the tables.

o   Put away the tables and chairs.

o   Empty, clean, and refill the coffee machine.

o   Count the used dishes and record the number of meals served on the client log sheet.

o   Fill and turn on the dishwasher.

o   Use a cloth to wash all of the sinks with soap and water, rinsing them clean.

o   Use disinfectant spray and a clean cloth to wipe down the countertops.

o   Make sure all of the appliances are unplugged and that the oven and stove elements are turned off.

o   Put all of the used towels and cloths into the washing machine.

o   Move laundry to dryer and turn it on.

o   Sign out. Thank you!

FRIDAY

Set-Up

o   Sign in.

o   Turn on washing machine.

o   Put out the tables and chairs.

o   Put out the plates, bowls, glasses, coffee cups (if you're serving coffee), spoons, and napkins.

o   If you're serving adults, turn the coffee maker on and put out milk and sugar for the coffee.

o   Put away the clean dishes.

o   Fold and put away the clean laundry.

o   Preheat the oven to 200°C (400°F).

o   Put out the milk, juice, and drinking water.

o   If you're using coffee carafes, fill and put them out.

o   Wash, slice, and put out the apples.

o   Put out two types of cereal—one regular and one gluten-free (today's alternate and gluten-free menu choices; Cheerios and Rice Krispies are gluten-free)—and milk.

o   Heat the banana bake you cut into squares yesterday (today's main menu choice) on the oven's top rack. Serve them immediately.

o   Move a bag of granola from the freezer to the refrigerator for Monday's breakfast. If the granola is getting low, make another batch.

Clean-Up

o   Use disinfectant spray and a clean cloth to wipe down the tables.

o   Put away the tables and chairs.

o   Empty, clean, and refill the coffee machine.

o   Count the used dishes and record the number of meals served on the client log sheet.

o   Fill and turn on the dishwasher.

o   Use a cloth to wash all of the sinks with soap and water, rinsing them clean.

o   Use disinfectant spray and a clean cloth to wipe down the countertops.

o   Make sure all of the appliances are unplugged and that the oven and stove elements are turned off.

o   Put all of the used towels and cloths into the washing machine.

o   Move laundry to dryer and turn it on.

o   Sign out. Thank you!

Week 3

MONDAY

Set-Up

o   Sign in.

o   Turn on washing machine.

o   Put out the tables and chairs.

o   Put out the plates, bowls, glasses, coffee cups (if you're serving coffee), spoons, and napkins.

o   If you're serving adults, turn the coffee maker on and put out milk and sugar for the coffee.

o   Put away the clean dishes.

o   Fold and put away the clean laundry.

o   Preheat the oven to 200°C (400°F).

o   Put out the drinking water.

o   If you're using coffee carafes, fill and put them out.

o   Wash, halve, and put out the bananas.

o   Put out two types of cereal (today's main menu choice) and milk.

o   Put out the yogurt and granola (today's alternate and gluten-free menu choices).

o   Mix and bake four dozen strawberry-swirl muffins for Wednesday's breakfast.

o   Slice, peel, and dice the ham for Tuesday's breakfast (ham-and-cheese quesadillas). Put the quesadillas together. Cover and place them in the refrigerator.

o   Move a bag of granola from the freezer to the refrigerator for Tuesday's breakfast. If the granola is getting low, make another batch.

Clean-Up
o   Use disinfectant spray and a clean cloth to wipe down the tables.
o   Put away the tables and chairs.
o   Empty, clean, and refill the coffee machine.
o   Count the used dishes and record the number of meals served on the client log sheet.
o   Fill and turn on the dishwasher.
o   Use a cloth to wash all of the sinks with soap and water, rinsing them clean.
o   Use disinfectant spray and a clean cloth to wipe down the countertops.
o   Make sure all of the appliances are unplugged and that the oven and stove elements are turned off.
o   Put all of the used towels and cloths into the washing machine.
o   Move laundry to dryer and turn it on.
o   Sign out. Thank you!

TUESDAY

Set-Up
o   Sign in.
o   Turn on washing machine.
o   Put out the tables and chairs.
o   Put out the plates, bowls, glasses, coffee cups (if you're serving coffee), knives, forks, spoons, and napkins.
o   If you're serving adults, turn the coffee maker on and put out milk and sugar for the coffee.
o   Put away the clean dishes.
o   Fold and put away the clean laundry.
o   Preheat the oven to 175°C (350°F).
o   Put out the milk and drinking water.

o   If you're using coffee carafes, fill and put them out.

o   Wash, slice, and put out the sweet peppers.

o   Use a griddle and nonstick frying pans to cook the ham-and-cheese quesadillas you prepared on Monday (today's main menu choice). Cut each quesadilla into six pieces. Put the pieces in a hotel pan and keep them warm in the oven until you're ready to serve them. Be sure to keep one or two gluten-free quesadilla portions (today's gluten-free menu choice) ready for anyone who needs it.

o   Put out the yogurt and granola (today's alternate menu choice). If the granola is getting low, make another batch.

o   Place a can of peaches in the refrigerator for Wednesday's breakfast.

Clean-Up

o   Use disinfectant spray and a clean cloth to wipe down the tables.

o   Put away the tables and chairs.

o   Empty, clean, and refill the coffee machine.

o   Count the used dishes and record the number of meals served on the client log sheet.

o   Fill and turn on the dishwasher.

o   Use a cloth to wash all of the sinks with soap and water, rinsing them clean.

o   Use disinfectant spray and a clean cloth to wipe down the countertops.

o   Make sure all of the appliances are unplugged and that the oven and stove elements are turned off.

o   Put all of the used towels and cloths into the washing machine.

o   Move laundry to dryer and turn it on.

o   Sign out. Thank you!

WEDNESDAY

Set-Up

o   Sign in.

o   Turn on washing machine.

o   Put out the tables and chairs.
o   Put out the plates, bowls, glasses, coffee cups (if you're serving coffee), spoons, and napkins.
o   If you're serving adults, turn the coffee maker on and put out milk and sugar for the coffee.
o   Put away the clean dishes.
o   Fold and put away the clean laundry.
o   Preheat the oven to 200°C (400°F).
o   Put out the milk and drinking water.
o   If you're using coffee carafes, fill and put them out.
o   Open the refrigerated can of peach slices. Portion the peaches into serving bowls and put them out.
o   Put out two types of cereal (one regular and one gluten-free— today's alternate and gluten-free menu choices; Cheerios and Rice Krispies are gluten-free) and milk.
o   Heat the strawberry-swirl muffins you baked on Monday (today's main menu choice) on the top rack of the oven. Serve them immediately.
o   Mix the batter for a loaded carrot bake for Friday's breakfast. Pour it into a four-inch-deep (10-centimetre) hotel pan that's been sprayed with oil and then lined with parchment paper. Cover and place the pan in the refrigerator.
o   Place any remaining strawberry-swirl muffins in a hotel pan in the freezer, so they can freeze individually.
o   Move a bag of granola from the freezer to the refrigerator for Thursday's breakfast. If the granola is getting low, make another batch.
o   Move six loaves of bread (including a gluten-free loaf) from the freezer to the back counter for Thursday's breakfast.

Clean-Up
o   Use disinfectant spray and a clean cloth to wipe down the tables.
o   Put away the tables and chairs.
o   Empty, clean, and refill the coffee machine.

o   Count the used dishes and record the number of meals served on the client log sheet.
o   Fill and turn on the dishwasher.
o   Use a cloth to wash all of the sinks with soap and water, rinsing them clean.
o   Use disinfectant spray and a clean cloth to wipe down the countertops.
o   Make sure all of the appliances are unplugged and that the oven and stove elements are turned off.
o   Put all of the used towels and cloths into the washing machine.
o   Move laundry to dryer and turn it on.
o   Sign out. Thank you!

THURSDAY

Set-Up
o   Sign in.
o   Turn on washing machine.
o   Put out the tables and chairs.
o   Put out the plates, bowls, glasses, coffee cups (if you're serving coffee), knives, spoons, and napkins.
o   If you're serving adults, turn the coffee maker on and put out milk and sugar for the coffee.
o   Put away the clean dishes.
o   Fold and put away the clean laundry.
o   Preheat the oven to 175°C (350°F).
o   Put out the juice.
o   If you're using coffee carafes, fill and put them out.
o   Wash, stem, and put out the cherry tomatoes.
o   Put out the honey, jam, and cream cheese for the toast.
o   Plug in and turn on the toaster. Start making toast (today's main menu choice) as soon as the toaster is hot. Keep a few slices of gluten-free bread available for those who need it.
o   Put out the yogurt and granola (today's alternate and gluten-free menu choices).

o   Bake the loaded carrot bake batter you mixed on Wednesday on the top rack of the oven. Cool, cover, and place it in the refrigerator for Friday's breakfast.

o   Move a bag of granola from the freezer to the refrigerator for Friday's breakfast. If the granola is getting low, make another batch.

o   Move Tuesday's frozen carrot-spice muffins from the hotel pan into labelled and dated ziplock bags. Place them back in the freezer.

Clean-Up

o   Use disinfectant spray and a clean cloth to wipe down the tables.

o   Put away the tables and chairs.

o   Empty, clean, and refill the coffee machine.

o   Count the used dishes and record the number of meals served on the client log sheet.

o   Fill and turn on the dishwasher.

o   Use a cloth to wash all of the sinks with soap and water, rinsing them clean.

o   Use disinfectant spray and a clean cloth to wipe down the countertops.

o   Make sure all of the appliances are unplugged and that the oven and stove elements are turned off.

o   Put all of the used towels and cloths into the washing machine.

o   Move laundry to dryer and turn it on.

o   Sign out. Thank you!

FRIDAY

Set-Up

o   Sign in.

o   Turn on washing machine.

o   Put out the tables and chairs.

o   Put out the plates, bowls, glasses, coffee cups (if you're serving coffee), forks, spoons, and napkins.

o   If you're serving adults, turn the coffee maker on and put out milk and sugar for the coffee.

o   Put away the clean dishes.

o   Fold and put away the clean laundry.

o   Turn oven on to 200°C (400°F).

o   Put out the milk and drinking water.

o   If you're using coffee carafes, fill and put them out.

o   Wash the grapes. Cut them into small bunches and put them out.

o   Cut the loaded carrot bake you baked on Thursday (today's main menu choice) into 45 pieces and place them on serving plates. Whip the cream and drop a dollop onto each piece of carrot bake. Serve immediately.

o   Put out the yogurt and granola (today's alternate and gluten-free menu choices).

o   If the granola is getting low, mix and bake another batch for Monday's breakfast. Allow it to cool, then put it in a labelled and dated ziplock bag and place it in the freezer.

o   Place an unopened can of fruit salad in the refrigerator for Monday's breakfast.

Clean-Up

o   Use disinfectant spray and a clean cloth to wipe down the tables.

o   Put away the tables and chairs.

o   Empty, clean, and refill the coffee machine.

o   Count the used dishes and record the number of meals served on the client log sheet.

o   Fill and turn on the dishwasher.

o   Use a cloth to wash all of the sinks with soap and water, rinsing them clean.

o   Use disinfectant spray and a clean cloth to wipe down the countertops.

o   Make sure all of the appliances are unplugged and that the oven and stove elements are turned off.

o   Put all of the used towels and cloths into the washing machine.

o   Move laundry to dryer and turn it on.

o   Sign out. Thank you!

Week 4

MONDAY

Set-Up
o   Sign in.
o   Turn on washing machine.
o   Put out the tables and chairs.
o   Put out the plates, bowls, glasses, coffee cups (if you're serving coffee), spoons, and napkins.
o   If you're serving adults, turn the coffee maker on and put out milk and sugar for the coffee.
o   Put away the clean dishes.
o   Fold and put away the clean laundry.
o   Put out the juice and drinking water.
o   If you're using coffee carafes, fill and put them out.
o   Open the refrigerated can of fruit salad. Portion the fruit salad into serving bowls and put them out.
o   Put out the yogurt and granola (today's main and gluten-free menu choices).
o   Put out two types of cereal (today's alternate menu choice) and milk.
o   Mix two batches of loaded chocolate bake batter for Wednesday's breakfast. Pour the batter into two four-inch-deep (10-centimetre) hotel pans that have been sprayed with oil and then lined with parchment paper. Cover and place the pans in the refrigerator.
o   Move a bag of granola from the freezer to the refrigerator for Tuesday's breakfast. If the granola is getting low, make another batch.
o   Move six loaves of bread (including a gluten-free loaf) from the freezer to the back counter for Thursday's breakfast.

Clean-Up

o   Use disinfectant spray and a clean cloth to wipe down the tables.

o   Put away the tables and chairs.

o   Empty, clean, and refill the coffee machine.

o   Count the used dishes and record the number of meals served on the client log sheet.

o   Fill and turn on the dishwasher.

o   Use a cloth to wash all of the sinks with soap and water, rinsing them clean.

o   Use disinfectant spray and a clean cloth to wipe down the countertops.

o   Make sure all of the appliances are unplugged and that the oven and stove elements are turned off.

o   Put all of the used towels and cloths into the washing machine.

o   Move laundry to dryer and turn it on.

o   Sign out. Thank you!

TUESDAY

Set-Up

o   Sign in.

o   Turn on washing machine.

o   Put out the tables and chairs.

o   Put out the plates, bowls, glasses, coffee cups (if you're serving coffee), knives, spoons, and napkins.

o   If you're serving adults, turn the coffee maker on and put out milk and sugar for the coffee.

o   Put away the clean dishes.

o   Fold and put away the clean laundry.

o   Preheat the oven to 175°C (350°F).

o   Put out the milk and drinking water.

o   If you're using coffee carafes, fill and put them out.

o   Wash, slice, and put out the apples.

o   Put out the honey, jam, and cream cheese for the toast.

o   Plug in and turn on the toaster. Start making toast (today's main and gluten-free menu choices) as soon as the toaster is hot. Keep a few slices of gluten-free bread available for those who need it.

o   Put out the yogurt and granola (today's alternate menu choice).

o   Bake the loaded chocolate bake batter you mixed on Monday. Partway through baking, rotate and switch the pans from the top to bottom racks. Then cool, cover, and place the pans in the refrigerator for Wednesday's breakfast.

Clean-Up

o   Use disinfectant spray and a clean cloth to wipe down the tables.

o   Put away the tables and chairs.

o   Empty, clean, and refill the coffee machine.

o   Count the used dishes and record the number of meals served on the client log sheet.

o   Fill and turn on the dishwasher.

o   Use a cloth to wash all of the sinks with soap and water, rinsing them clean.

o   Use disinfectant spray and a clean cloth to wipe down the countertops.

o   Make sure all of the appliances are unplugged and that the oven and stove elements are turned off.

o   Put all of the used towels and cloths into the washing machine.

o   Move laundry to dryer and turn it on.

o   Sign out. Thank you!

WEDNESDAY

Set-Up

o   Sign in.

o   Turn on washing machine.

o   Put out the tables and chairs.

o   Put out the plates, bowls, glasses, coffee cups (if you're serving coffee), forks, spoons, and napkins.

o   If you're serving adults, turn the coffee maker on and put out milk and sugar for the coffee.
o   Put away the clean dishes.
o   Fold and put away the clean laundry.
o   Put out the milk and drinking water.
o   If you're using coffee carafes, fill and put them out.
o   Wash, peel, cut, and put out the carrots.
o   Make the icing for the loaded chocolate bake (today's main menu choice). Ice the two chocolate bakes and cut each one into 45 pieces. Put them out on serving plates.
o   Put out two types of cereal (one regular and one gluten-free— today's alternate and gluten-free menu choices; Cheerios and Rice Krispies are gluten-free) and milk.
o   Mix the batter for a fruit loaf for Friday's breakfast. Pour the batter into a four-inch-deep (10-centimetre) hotel pan that's been sprayed with oil and then lined with parchment paper. Cover and place the pan in the refrigerator.

Clean-Up
o   Use disinfectant spray and a clean cloth to wipe down the tables.
o   Put away the tables and chairs.
o   Empty, clean, and refill the coffee machine.
o   Count the used dishes and record the number of meals served on the client log sheet.
o   Fill and turn on the dishwasher.
o   Use a cloth to wash all of the sinks with soap and water, rinsing them clean.
o   Use disinfectant spray and a clean cloth to wipe down the countertops.
o   Make sure all of the appliances are unplugged and that the oven and stove elements are turned off.
o   Put all of the used towels and cloths into the washing machine.
o   Move laundry to dryer and turn it on.
o   Sign out. Thank you!

THURSDAY

Set-Up

o Sign in.

o Turn on washing machine.

o Put out the tables and chairs.

o Put out the plates, bowls, glasses, coffee cups (if you're serving coffee), spoons, and napkins.

o If you're serving adults, turn the coffee maker on and put out milk and sugar for the coffee.

o Put away the clean dishes.

o Fold and put away the clean laundry.

o Preheat the oven to 175°C (350°F).

o Put out the drinking water.

o If you're using coffee carafes, fill and put them out.

o Prepare and serve the Shrek smoothies.

o Put out the granola bars (today's main menu choice).

o Move a bag of strawberry-swirl muffins (today's alternate menu choice) from the freezer to the refrigerator. When someone asks for a muffin, microwave it for about thirty seconds before serving it.

o Put out gluten-free cereal (today's gluten-free menu choice; Cheerios and Rice Krispies are gluten-free) and milk.

o Bake the fruit loaf you mixed on Wednesday. Cool, cover, and place the fruit loaf in the refrigerator for Friday's breakfast.

o Move a bag of granola from the freezer to the refrigerator for Friday's breakfast. If the granola is getting low, make another batch.

o If any strawberry-swirl muffins are left over from today's breakfast, put them back in the freezer.

Clean-Up

o Use disinfectant spray and a clean cloth to wipe down the tables.

o Put away the tables and chairs.

o Empty, clean, and refill the coffee machine.

- o Count the used dishes and record the number of meals served on the client log sheet.
- o Fill and turn on the dishwasher.
- o Use a cloth to wash all of the sinks with soap and water, rinsing them clean.
- o Use disinfectant spray and a clean cloth to wipe down the countertops.
- o Make sure all of the appliances are unplugged and that the oven and stove elements are turned off.
- o Put all of the used towels and cloths into the washing machine.
- o Move laundry to dryer and turn it on.
- o Sign out. Thank you!

FRIDAY

Set-Up
- o Sign in.
- o Turn on washing machine.
- o Put out the tables and chairs.
- o Put out the plates, bowls, glasses, coffee cups (if you're serving coffee), forks, spoons, and napkins.
- o If you're serving adults, turn the coffee maker on and put out milk and sugar for the coffee.
- o Put away the clean dishes.
- o Fold and put away the clean laundry.
- o Put out the milk and drinking water.
- o If you're using coffee carafes, fill and put them out.
- o Wash, slice, and put out the oranges.
- o Slice and put out the fruit loaf you baked yesterday (today's main menu choice).
- o Put out the yogurt and granola (today's alternate and gluten-free menu choices).
- o Move a bag of granola from the freezer to the refrigerator for Monday's breakfast. If the granola is getting low, make another batch.

Clean-Up

o   Use disinfectant spray and a clean cloth to wipe down the tables.

o   Put away the tables and chairs.

o   Empty, clean, and refill the coffee machine.

o   Count the used dishes and record the number of meals served on the client log sheet.

o   Fill and turn on the dishwasher.

o   Use a cloth to wash all of the sinks with soap and water, rinsing them clean.

o   Use disinfectant spray and a clean cloth to wipe down the countertops.

o   Make sure all of the appliances are unplugged and that the oven and stove elements are turned off.

o   Put all of the used towels and cloths into the washing machine.

o   Move laundry to dryer and turn it on.

o   Sign out. Thank you!

Week 5

MONDAY

Set-Up

o   Sign in.

o   Turn on washing machine.

o   Put out the tables and chairs.

o   Put out the plates, bowls, glasses, coffee cups (if you're serving coffee), spoons, and napkins.

o   If you're serving adults, turn the coffee maker on and put out milk and sugar for the coffee.

o   Put away the clean dishes.

o   Fold and put away the clean laundry.

o   Preheat the oven to 200°C (400°F).

o   Put out the drinking water.

○ If you're using coffee carafes, fill and put them out.

○ Wash, halve, and put out the bananas.

○ Put out two types of cereal (one regular and one gluten-free—today's main and gluten-free menu choices; Cheerios and Rice Krispies are gluten-free) and milk.

○ Put out the yogurt and granola (today's alternate menu choice).

○ Mix and bake four dozen blueberry-crumble muffins for Tuesday's breakfast. Cool, cover, and place the muffins in the refrigerator.

○ Move a bag of granola from the freezer to the refrigerator for Tuesday's breakfast. If the granola is getting low, make another batch.

○ Mix the batter for breakfast bread for Wednesday's breakfast. Pour the batter into two hotel pans that's been sprayed with oil and then lined with parchment. Cover and place the pans in the refrigerator.

Clean-Up

○ Use disinfectant spray and a clean cloth to wipe down the tables.

○ Put away the tables and chairs.

○ Empty, clean, and refill the coffee machine.

○ Count the used dishes and record the number of meals served on the client log sheet.

○ Fill and turn on the dishwasher.

○ Use a cloth to wash all of the sinks with soap and water, rinsing them clean.

○ Use disinfectant spray and a clean cloth to wipe down the countertops.

○ Make sure all of the appliances are unplugged and that the oven and stove elements are turned off.

○ Put all of the used towels and cloths into the washing machine.

○ Move laundry to dryer and turn it on.

○ Sign out. Thank you!

TUESDAY

Set-Up

o   Sign in.
o   Turn on washing machine.
o   Put out the tables and chairs.
o   Put out the plates, bowls, glasses, coffee cups (if you're serving coffee), spoons, and napkins.
o   If you're serving adults, turn the coffee maker on and put out milk and sugar for the coffee.
o   Put away the clean dishes.
o   Fold and put away the clean laundry.
o   Preheat the oven to 200°C (400°F).
o   Put out the milk and drinking water.
o   If you're using coffee carafes, fill and put them out.
o   Place the raisins in a serving dish with a spoon and put them out.
o   Heat the blueberry-crumble muffins (today's main menu choice) on the top shelf of the oven. Serve them immediately.
o   Put out the yogurt and granola (today's alternate and gluten-free menu choices).
o   Bake the breakfast bread you mixed yesterday. Cool, cover, and store it in the refrigerator for Wednesday's breakfast.
o   Place any remaining blueberry-crumble muffins in a hotel pan in the freezer, so they can freeze individually.

Clean-Up

o   Use disinfectant spray and a clean cloth to wipe down the tables.
o   Put away the tables and chairs.
o   Empty, clean, and refill the coffee machine.
o   Count the used dishes and record the number of meals served on the client log sheet.
o   Fill and turn on the dishwasher.

- o   Use a cloth to wash all of the sinks with soap and water, rinsing them clean.
- o   Use disinfectant spray and a clean cloth to wipe down the countertops.
- o   Make sure all of the appliances are unplugged and that the oven and stove elements are turned off.
- o   Put all of the used towels and cloths into the washing machine.
- o   Move laundry to dryer and turn it on.
- o   Sign out. Thank you!

WEDNESDAY

Set-Up

- o   Sign in.
- o   Turn on washing machine.
- o   Put out the tables and chairs.
- o   Put out the plates, bowls, glasses, coffee cups (if you're serving coffee), knives, forks, spoons, and napkins.
- o   If you're serving adults, turn the coffee maker on and put out milk and sugar for the coffee.
- o   Put away the clean dishes.
- o   Fold and put away the clean laundry.
- o   Preheat the oven on to 200°C (400°F).
- o   Put out the milk, juice, and drinking water.
- o   If you're using coffee carafes, fill and put them out.
- o   Wash, cut, and put out the celery.
- o   Arrange the ham and the cheese on top of the breakfast bread you prepared yesterday (today's main menu choice). Heat it on the top shelf of the oven until the cheese melts. Serve the breakfast bread immediately.
- o   Put out two types of cereal (one regular and one gluten-free—today's alternate and gluten-free menu choices; Cheerios and Rice Krispies are gluten-free) and milk.
- o   Mix a batch of pumpkin-spice pancake batter for Friday's breakfast. Cover and place the batter in the refrigerator.

o　Move a bag of granola from the freezer to the refrigerator for Thursday's breakfast. If the granola is getting low, make another batch.

o　Move six loaves of bread (including a gluten-free loaf) from the freezer to the back counter for Thursday's breakfast.

o　Move Wednesday's frozen blueberry-crumble muffins from the hotel pan into labelled and dated ziplock bags. Place them back in the freezer.

Clean-Up

o　Use disinfectant spray and a clean cloth to wipe down the tables.

o　Put away the tables and chairs.

o　Empty, clean, and refill the coffee machine.

o　Count the used dishes and record the number of meals served on the client log sheet.

o　Fill and turn on the dishwasher.

o　Use a cloth to wash all of the sinks with soap and water, rinsing them clean.

o　Use disinfectant spray and a clean cloth to wipe down the countertops.

o　Make sure all of the appliances are unplugged and that the oven and stove elements are turned off.

o　Put all of the used towels and cloths into the washing machine.

o　Move laundry to dryer and turn it on.

o　Sign out. Thank you!

THURSDAY

Set-Up

o　Sign in.

o　Turn on washing machine.

o　Put out the tables and chairs.

o　Put out the plates, bowls, glasses, coffee cups (if you're serving coffee), knives, spoons, and napkins.

- If you're serving adults, turn the coffee maker on and put out milk and sugar for the coffee.
- Put away the clean dishes.
- Fold and put away the clean laundry.
- Put out the milk and drinking water.
- If you're using coffee carafes, fill and put them out.
- Wash the melons and remove the seeds. Cut the melons into slices and put them out.
- Put out the honey, jam, and cream cheese for the toast.
- Plug in and turn on the toaster. Start making toast (today's main and gluten-free menu choices) as soon as the toaster is hot. Keep a few slices of gluten-free bread available for those who need it.
- Put out the yogurt and granola (today's alternate menu choice).
- Use a griddle and nonstick frying pans to cook the pumpkin-spice pancake batter you made on Wednesday. Cover and store the pancakes in the refrigerator for Friday's breakfast.
- Place an unopened can of fruit salad in the refrigerator for Friday's breakfast.

Clean-Up
- Use disinfectant spray and a clean cloth to wipe down the tables.
- Put away the tables and chairs.
- Empty, clean, and refill the coffee machine.
- Count the used dishes and record the number of meals served on the client log sheet.
- Fill and turn on the dishwasher.
- Use a cloth to wash all of the sinks with soap and water, rinsing them clean.
- Use disinfectant spray and a clean cloth to wipe down the countertops.
- Make sure all of the appliances are unplugged and that the oven and stove elements are turned off.
- Put all of the used towels and cloths into the washing machine.

o   Move laundry to dryer and turn it on.
o   Sign out. Thank you!

FRIDAY

Set-Up
o   Sign in.
o   Turn on washing machine,
o   Put out the tables and chairs.
o   Put out the plates, bowls, glasses, coffee cups (if you're serving coffee), forks, spoons, and napkins.
o   If you're serving adults, turn the coffee maker on and put out milk and sugar for the coffee.
o   Put away the clean dishes.
o   Fold and put away the clean laundry.
o   Put out the milk, juice, and drinking water.
o   If you're using coffee carafes, fill and put them out.
o   Open the refrigerated can of fruit salad. Portion the fruit salad into serving bowls and put them out.
o   Put out the syrup for the pancakes.
o   Preheat the oven to 200°C (400°F).
o   Cut up the pumpkin-spice pancakes (today's main and gluten-free menu choices) and heat them on the top shelf of the oven. Keep the gluten-free pancake mix, the pumpkin, and the spices available, and make gluten-free pancakes to order for those who need them.
o   Put out two types of cereal (today's alternate menu choice) and milk.
o   Move six loaves of bread (including a gluten-free loaf) from the freezer to the back counter for Monday's breakfast.

Clean-Up
o   Use disinfectant spray and a clean cloth to wipe down the tables.
o   Put away the tables and chairs.

o   Empty, clean, and refill the coffee machine.
o   Count the used dishes and record the number of meals served on the client log sheet.
o   Fill and turn on the dishwasher.
o   Use a cloth to wash all of the sinks with soap and water, rinsing them clean.
o   Use disinfectant spray and a clean cloth to wipe down the countertops.
o   Make sure all of the appliances are unplugged and that the oven and stove elements are turned off.
o   Put all of the used towels and cloths into the washing machine.
o   Move laundry to dryer and turn it on.
o   Sign out. Thank you!

Appendix D

Weekly Ordering Sheets
for a Five-Week Menu Plan

The following ordering sheets are based on the menu plan given in Appendix A for a sit-down daily breakfast program with a five-week menu rotation for children, preteens or seniors. If you are ordering for teenagers or adults, it is best to double the ingredients on the lists.

These ordering sheets are intended to be used as reference checklists, to be sure you have everything you need to prepare your menu items for the week.

Each order must be placed in time to arrive *before* Monday of the week listed on the ordering sheet. That is, you'll need to place the first Week 1 order the week before your program launches, then place the Week 2 order during Week 1, place the Week 3 order during Week 2, and so on.

You'll see that staples, dry goods, and cleaning supplies are listed only for Week 1. You'll need to check your stock each week, however, and reorder these items when they run low.

Note that the quantities available at your grocery store may differ from those listed here. Just get the closest you can.

Week 1

MEAT
____ 1 toupie ham

DAIRY
____ 5 (4-litre/1-gallon) jugs whole (homogenized) milk
____ 2 (500-gram/17.6-ounce) containers cream cheese
____ 1 dozen eggs
____ 1 large tub margarine
____ 4 large tubs vanilla yogurt (NOT plain yogurt)
____ 1 large bag shredded cheddar cheese

PRODUCE
____ 3 English cucumbers
____ 25 bananas
____ 12 oranges
____ 11 apples
____ 1 (453-gram/1-pound) bag carrots
____ 4 (1-litre/1-quart) containers orange or apple juice
____ 1 bottle lemon juice

BREAD AND CEREAL
____ 5 loaves whole-grain bread
____ 1 loaf gluten-free bread (or more, depending on how many gluten-sensitive clients you have)
____ 4 dozen whole-grain buns
____ 1 dozen gluten-free buns (or more, depending on how many gluten-sensitive clients you have)
____ 2 jumbo boxes Rice Krispies (which are naturally gluten-free)
____ 1 jumbo box Shreddies

___ 1 jumbo box Corn Flakes

___ 1 jumbo box Cheerios

___ 1 (900-gram/32-ounce) bag gluten-free quick-cooking rolled oats

___ 6 bags bran muffin mix

CANNED GOODS

___ 1 (3-kilogram/106-ounce) can fruit salad

STAPLES

___ 1 (3-kilogram/6.6-pound) container liquid honey

___ 1 (1-kilogram/2.2-pound) container creamed honey

___ 2 (1-litre/1-quart) jars strawberry or raspberry jam

___ 1 (1-litre/1-quart) container vegetable oil (to blend with olive oil)

___ 1 (1-litre/1-quart) bottle extra-virgin olive oil (to blend with vegetable oil)

___ 1 large can cooking spray

___ 1 (1-litre/1-quart) bottle vanilla

___ 1 (5-kilogram/11-pound) bag unbleached flour

___ 1 (2.5-kilogram/5.5-pound) bag whole wheat flour

___ 1 (1-kilogram/2.2-pound) bag brown or golden-yellow sugar

___ 1 (1-kilogram/2.2-pound) container icing sugar

___ 1 (1.5-kilogram/3.3-pound) bag of white sugar

___ 1 (454-gram/16-ounce) container of baking soda

___ 1 (230-gram/8-ounce) container baking powder

___ 1 (510-gram/18-ounce) container cinnamon

___ 1 (45-gram/1.5-ounce) container ground nutmeg

___ 1 (45-gram/1.5-ounce) container allspice

___ 1 (45-gram/1.5-ounce) container ground cloves

DRY GOODS

___ 3 boxes large ziplock freezer bags

___ 2 boxes medium ziplock freezer bags

___ 2 rolls parchment paper

___ 1 roll plastic wrap (e.g., Saran Wrap, Glad Wrap)

___ 1 roll aluminum foil

___ 6 rolls paper towels

___ 5,000 napkins

CLEANING SUPPLIES

___ 1 (3-litre/102-ounce) bottle liquid dish soap

___ 90 portions dishwasher detergent

___ 5 large bottles hand sanitizer

___ 1 (3.78-litre/128-ounce) bottle multi-surface cleaner and disinfectant

___ 12 dish cloths or cleaning cloths

___ 12 dish towels

___ 3 sponges with scrubbies

___ 1 apron per person

Week 2

MEAT

___ 2 packages unsliced bacon (to be cut into cubes)

DAIRY

___ 4 (4-litre/1-gallon) jugs whole (homogenized) milk

___ 2 (226-gram/8-ounce) bags shredded cheddar cheese

___ 2 (500-gram/17.6-ounce) containers cream cheese

___ 2 dozen eggs

___ 1 large tub margarine

___ 2 large tubs vanilla yogurt (NOT plain yogurt)

PRODUCE

___ 12 oranges

___ 8 carrots

___ 11 apples

___ 25 ripe bananas

___ 2 large bunches fresh or 1 small package frozen kale

___ 2 (2.75-kilogram/6-pound) packages frozen mixed fruit

___ 1 (2.75-kilogram/6-pound) package frozen strawberries

___ 1 (907-gram/2-pound) package frozen **OR** 750 millilitres (3 cups) fresh blueberries

___ 4 (1-litre/1-quart) containers orange or apple juice

BREAD AND CEREAL

___ 5 loaves whole-grain bread

___ 1 loaf gluten-free bread (or more, depending on how many gluten-sensitive clients you have)

___ 2 jumbo boxes Rice Krispies (which are naturally gluten-free)

___ 1 jumbo box Shreddies

___ 1 jumbo box Corn Flakes

___ 1 jumbo box Cheerios

___ 1 (900-gram/31.8-ounce) bag gluten-free rolled oats

___ 6 bags commercial muffin mix

___ 7 boxes fruit granola bars (8 bars per box)

CANNED GOODS

___ 1 (3-kilogram/106-ounce) can fruit salad

___ 2 (796-millilitre/27-ounce) jars apple sauce

STAPLES

Check your stock to see what you need to reorder.

DRY GOODS

Check your stock to see what you need to reorder.

CLEANING SUPPLIES

Check your stock to see what you need to reorder.

Week 3

MEAT
- ____ 1 toupie ham

DAIRY
- ____ 4 (4-litre/1-gallon) jugs whole (homogenized) milk
- ____ 1 (1-litre/1-quart) container whipping cream
- ____ 3 (500-gram/17.6-ounce) containers cream cheese
- ____ 2 dozen eggs
- ____ 1 large tub margarine
- ____ 5 large tubs vanilla yogurt (NOT plain yogurt)
- ____ 2 bags shredded cheddar cheese

PRODUCE
- ____ 28 bananas
- ____ 6 sweet peppers (red, green, yellow, and/or orange)
- ____ 3 baskets cherry tomatoes
- ____ 3 large bunches grapes
- ____ 8 carrots
- ____ 3 zucchinis
- ____ 4 (1-litre/1-quart) containers orange or apple juice

BREAD AND CEREAL
- ____ 5 loaves whole-grain bread
- ____ 1 loaf gluten-free bread (or more, depending on how many gluten-sensitive clients you have)
- ____ 4 packages whole-wheat tortillas (each containing 10 tortillas)
- ____ 2 jumbo boxes Rice Krispies (which are naturally gluten-free)
- ____ 1 jumbo box Shreddies
- ____ 1 jumbo box Corn Flakes
- ____ 1 jumbo box Cheerios
- ____ 1 (900-gram/31.8-ounce) bag gluten-free rolled oats

___ 9 (900-gram/31.8-ounce) bags of generic oatmeal or bran muffin mix

CANNED GOODS

___ 1 (3-kilogram/106-ounce) can peach slices
___ 1 (3-kilogram/106-ounce) can fruit salad
___ 2 (50-gram/19-ounce) cans crushed pineapple

STAPLES

Check your stock to see what you need to reorder.

DRY GOODS

Check your stock to see what you need to reorder.

CLEANING SUPPLIES

Check your stock to see what you need to reorder.

Week 4

MEAT

___ None.

DAIRY

___ 4 (4-litre/1-gallon) jugs whole (homogenized) milk
___ 2 (500-gram/17.6-ounce) containers cream cheese
___ 2 dozen eggs
___ 1 large tub margarine
___ 2 large tubs vanilla yogurt (NOT plain yogurt)

PRODUCE

___ 11 apples
___ 1 large bag carrots
___ 2 lare bunches fresh or 1 small bag frozen kale

___ 2 (2.75-kilogram/6-pound) packages frozen mixed fruit

___ 1 (2-kilogram/4-pound) package frozen strawberries

___ 12 oranges

___ 4 (1-litre/1-quart) containers orange or apple juice

BREAD AND CEREAL

___ 5 loaves whole-grain bread

___ 1 loaf gluten-free bread (or more, depending on how many gluten-sensitive clients you have)

___ 2 jumbo boxes Rice Krispies (which are naturally gluten-free)

___ 1 jumbo box Shreddies

___ 1 jumbo box Corn Flakes

___ 1 jumbo box Cheerios

___ 1 (900-gram/31.8-ounce) package gluten-free rolled oats

___ 7 boxes granola bars (8 per box)

___ 9 (900-gram/31.8-ounce) bags of generic oatmeal or bran muffin mix

CANNED GOODS

___ 3 (454-millilitre/15-ounce) cans puréed pumpkin

___ 1 (3-kilogram/106-ounce) can fruit salad

STAPLES

Check your stock to see what you need to reorder.

DRY GOODS

Check your stock to see what you need to reorder.

CLEANING SUPPLIES

Check your stock to see what you need to reorder.

Week 5

MEAT
____ 1 toupie ham

DAIRY
____ 4 (4-litre/1-gallon) jugs whole (homogenized) milk
____ 2 (500-gram/17.6-ounce) containers cream cheese
____ 1 dozen eggs
____ 1 large tub margarine
____ 4 large tubs vanilla yogurt (NOT plain yogurt)

PRODUCE
____ 25 bananas
____ 1 large bag raisins (from a nut-free facility)
____ 1 bunch celery
____ 2 melons, any type (cantaloupe, honeydew, muskmelon, etc.), **OR** 1 watermelon
____ 1 (450-gram/1-pound) package frozen **OR** 500 millilitres (2 cups) fresh blueberries
____ 4 (1-litre/1-quart) containers orange or apple juice

BREAD AND CEREAL
____ 5 loaves whole-grain bread
____ 1 loaf gluten-free bread (or more, depending on how many gluten-sensitive clients you have)
____ 2 jumbo boxes Rice Krispies (which are naturally gluten-free)
____ 1 jumbo box Shreddies
____ 1 jumbo box Corn Flakes
____ 1 jumbo box Cheerios
____ 1 (900-gram/31.8-ounce) bag gluten-free rolled oats

CANNED GOODS
____ 3 (454-millilitre/15-ounce) cans puréed pumpkin

STAPLES

Check your stock to see what you need to reorder.

DRY GOODS

Check your stock to see what you need to reorder.

CLEANING SUPPLIES

Check your stock to see what you need to reorder.

Appendix E

Food Safety Sheets and Refrigerator/Freezer Temperature Audit Form

Food Safety Sheets

When starting up your kitchen, it is important to first check with your local food health and safety committee to see what the safe holding temperatures are in your area. Many places will be different than others. Ensure that the following food safety sheets are in your procedures binder, readily accessible to paid and volunteer personnel.

Make sure all of your paid and volunteer staff are familiar with them. It's also a good idea to post them prominently in the kitchen.

FOOD SAFETY FOR CASSEROLES

Receiving
- Receive all ingredients from approved sources.

- Check and smell the ingredients before using them.
- Thoroughly wash the ingredients.

Preparation and Handling

- Wash your hands.
- Clean and disinfect all work surfaces, utensils, and cutting boards after each use.
- Follow the recipes carefully.
- Casseroles should be served within two hours of cooking.
- Discard any items that sit at room temperature for more than two hours.

Cooking

- Cook casseroles until internal temperatures are at least 165°F (74°C) for ten minutes or more, then hold them at 140°F (60°C).

Hot or Cold Holding

- Keep hot casseroles at 140°F (60°C) for up to two hours.
- Keep refrigerated casseroles at less than 40°F (4°C) for up to three days.
- Discard any food that's held for longer than two hours at less than 140°F (60°C).

Cooling

- Cool casseroles to 68°F (20°C) within two hours, then to 40°F (4°C) within four more hours.
- Store casseroles at 40°F (4°C) for up to three days.
- Discard any food that's not cooled to these temperatures.

Delivery to Clients

- Keep hot casseroles at 140°F (60°C) or a little more during delivery.
- Keep cold casseroles at less than 40°F (4°C) during delivery.

Storage and Thawing

- Refrigerate casseroles at 40°F (4°C) or less.
- Freeze casseroles at less than 0°F (−18°C).
- Thaw casseroles in the refrigerator.

Reheating

- Reheat casseroles until they reach 165°F (74°C) and maintain that temperature for ten to twenty minutes before removing them from the oven.
- Hold hot casseroles at 140°F (60°C) for up to two hours.
- Discard any reheated leftovers.

Daily Monitoring

- Check oven, refrigerator, and freezer temperatures.
- Monitor production times.
- Monitor storage times.

FOOD SAFETY FOR DAIRY PRODUCTS

Receiving

- Receive all dairy products from approved sources.
- Thoroughly inspect dairy product containers and packaging before placing them in the refrigerator or freezer.
- Check and smell dairy products before using them.

Storage

- Refrigerate dairy products at 40°F (4°C) or less.
- Freeze daily products at less than 0°F (−18°C).
- Thaw dairy products in the refrigerator.
- Rotate the dairy products; use the oldest products first.
- Leave dairy products in their original containers. If left open, they can pick up odours and flavours from other foods in the refrigerator.
- Never add an old dairy product to a new dairy product.

Preparation and Handling
- Wash your hands.
- Clean and disinfect all work surfaces, utensils, and cutting boards after each use.
- Minimize preparation time, so dairy products remain cold.
- Keep dairy products out of the refrigerator or freezer just long enough to use and serve them. Return them to the refrigerator or freezer as soon as possible.

Delivery
- Keep refrigerated dairy products at 40°F (4°C) or less during delivery.
- Keep frozen dairy products at less than 0°F (−18°C) during delivery.

Daily Monitoring
- Check refrigerator and freezer temperatures.
- Monitor production times.
- Monitor storage times.

FOOD SAFETY FOR DESSERTS

Receiving
- Receive all ingredients from approved sources.
- Thoroughly check all packaging.
- Check and smell all ingredients before using them.

Storage and Thawing
- Refrigerate desserts at 40°F (4°C) or less.
- Freeze desserts at less than 0°F (−18°C).
- Thaw desserts in the refrigerator.
- Store fruit pies, cookies, dry cakes, and dry pastries at room temperature.

- Refrigerate all other desserts, including pies or cakes that contain custard or pumpkin.

Preparation and Handling

- Wash your hands.
- Clean and sanitize all work surfaces, utensils, and cutting boards after each use.
- Follow the recipes carefully.
- Desserts should be prepared in less than two hours.
- Bring desserts out of the refrigerator for portioning and garnishing, if necessary, then return them to the refrigerator until you serve them.
- Discard any perishable items (ingredients or finished desserts) that sit at room temperature for more than two hours.

Cooling

- Cool perishable desserts to 68°F (20°C) within two hours, then to 40°F (4°C) within another four hours.
- Discard any perishable desserts that are not cooled to these temperatures.
- Store desserts for up to three days.

Delivery

- Keep refrigerated desserts at 40°F (4°C) or less during delivery.
- Keep frozen desserts at less than 0°F (−18°C) during delivery.

Daily Monitoring

- Check refrigerator, freezer, and oven temperatures.
- Monitor production times.
- Monitor storage times.
- Discard any custards, puddings, cheesecakes, Bavarian creams, mousses, sherbets, parfaits, bread puddings, and rice puddings that are not handled properly, as outlined above.

FOOD SAFETY FOR FRUITS AND VEGETABLES

Receiving
- Receive all fruits and vegetables from approved sources.
- Check and smell all fruits and vegetables before using them.
- Thoroughly wash all fruits and vegetables. If they're packaged, wash their packaging.
- Discard any fruits and vegetables that are discoloured or unappealing.

Storage and Thawing
- Refrigerate fruits and vegetables at 40°F (4°C) or less.
- Freeze fruits and vegetables at less than 0°F (−18°C).
- Thaw fruits and vegetables in the refrigerator.

Preparation and Handling
- Wash your hands.
- Clean and disinfect all work surfaces, utensils, and cutting boards after each use.
- Follow any recipes carefully.
- Fruits and vegetables should be prepared in less than two hours.
- Discard any cut and prepared fruits and vegetables that sit at room temperature for more than two hours.

Salads
- Soak cut lettuce in cold water in a clean container. Drain and rinse. Refrigerate in a clean, covered container.
- If adding ingredients such as mayonnaise, treat salads as a high-risk food. Keep them refrigerated at 40°F (4°C) or less.
- Immediately refrigerate leftover salads.

Fruits and Vegetables
- Remove any inedible parts and peel and rinse.
- Store fruits and vegetables in clean inserts in a designated area of the refrigerator at 40°F (4°C) or less.

- Wash berries and grapes under cold running water. Air-dry them in a colander.
- Portion any fruits used for desserts. Place them in the refrigerator until serving time.

Delivery
- Keep refrigerated fruits and vegetables (and foods containing them) at 40°F (4°C) or less during delivery.
- Keep frozen fruits and vegetables at less than 0°F (−18°C) during delivery.

Daily Monitoring
- Check refrigerator, freezer, and oven temperatures.
- Monitor production times.
- Monitor storage times.

FOOD SAFETY FOR PROCESSED MEATS

Receiving
- Receive all processed meats from approved sources.
- Ensure that both fresh and frozen processed meats arrive in sealed packaging.
- Thorough inspect all packaging by checking for tears and tampering.
- Check and smell any processed meats before using them.

Storage and Thawing
- Refrigerate processed meats at 40°F (4°C) or less.
- Freeze processed meats at less than 0°F (−18°C).
- Thaw processed meats in the refrigerator.

Preparation and Handling
- Wash your hands frequently.

- Clean and disinfect all work surfaces, utensils, and cutting boards after each use.
- Carefully follow any recipes.
- Meals containing processed meats should be prepared in less than two hours.
- Discard any processed meats that sit at room temperature for more than two hours.
- Wear disposable gloves when slicing, cutting, or chopping processed meats. Handle processed meats as little as possible.
- Refrigerate processed meats at 40°F (4°C).

Delivery

- Keep refrigerated items containing processed meats at 40°F (4°C) or less during delivery.
- Keep frozen items containing processed meats at less than 0°F (−18°C) during delivery.

Daily Monitoring

- Check refrigerator and freezer temperatures.
- Monitor production times.
- Monitor storage times.

FOOD SAFETY FOR ROASTED MEATS

Receiving

- Receive all raw and roasted meats from approved sources.
- Thoroughly inspect all packaging for tears or tampering.
- Check and smell all raw and roasted meats before using them.

Preparation and Handling

- Wash your hands.
- Clean and disinfect all work surfaces, utensils, cutting boards, and meat thermometers after each use.

- Carefully follow any recipes.
- Discard any raw or roasted meats that sit at room temperature for more than two hours.

Cooking

- Use a thermometer to check for internal temperatures.
- Cook roast beef, lamb, pork, ham, and ground beef until internal temperatures reach 158°F (70°C).
- Cook poultry, including stuffing, until internal temperatures reach 165°F (74°C).
- Cook fish until internal temperatures reach 158°F (70°C).
- When the meat has finished cooking, remove it from the oven and let it rest for five minutes, until it reaches a temperature suitable for slicing.

Hot or Cold Holding

- Keep hot meats at 165°F (74°C) or more for up to two hours. Do not let the holding temperature fall below 140°F (40°C).
- Keep refrigerated meats at 40°F (4°C) or less for up to 48 hours.

Cooling

- Cool roasted meats to 68°F (20°C) within two hours, then to 40°F (4°C) within another four hours.
- Discard any roasted meats that are not cooled to these specifications.
- Store roasted meats in the refrigerator for up to three days.

Reheating

- Reheat roasted meats to 165°F (74°C) within a two-hour period, then hold them at that temperature for ten to twenty minutes before serving.
- Keep roasted meats at 140°F (60°C) for up to two hours.
- Discard any reheated leftovers.

Delivery

- Keep cold roasted meats at 40°F (4°C) or less during delivery.
- Keep hot roasted meats at 140°F (60°C) or a little more for up to two hours.
- Keep frozen roasted meats at less than 0°F (−18°C) during delivery.

Daily Monitoring

- Check refrigerator, freezer, and oven temperatures.
- Monitor production times.
- Monitor storage times.

Refrigerator/Freezer Temperature Audit Form

Include the following form in your procedures binder. Ensure that all of your paid and volunteer staff are familiar with it.

You might want to assign the task of recording these temperatures every day to a specific person.

[NAME OF PROGRAM]
REFRIGERATOR AND FREEZER TEMPERATURES

Month _____ Year _____

Please record the temperatures and sign your initials in the columns beside them.

Morning volunteers must record each temperature daily.

The standard temperature for the freezer is −18°C (0°F). The standard temperature for the fridge is 4°C (40°F).

If the actual temperatures vary from these standards by 5° or more, please inform the program coordinator immediately.

Date	AM Refrigerator Temperature	Your Initials	AM Freezer Temperature	Your Initials
1				
2				
3				
4				
5				
6				
7				
8				
9				
10				
11				
12				
13				
14				
15				
16				
17				

Date	AM Refrigerator Temperature	Your Initials	AM Freezer Temperature	Your Initials
18				
19				
20				
21				
22				
23				
24				
25				
26				
27				
28				
29				
30				
31				

Appendix F

Personnel Forms

The forms on the following pages are provided for your convenience. You can customize them to meet the needs of your specific program.

Criminal-Record Check

It's important to do a criminal-record check for everyone who works with a marginalized population—especially if your clients are children.

Have each paid or volunteer staff member sign this agreement. Provide him or her with a copy of the signed agreement.

Keep all of the original signed agreements, together with your notes, in your confidential personnel binder.

SAFETY CHECK APPLICATION

Program _____

Facility _____

Name

Address

Home phone

Mobile phone

Email

Have you ever been convicted of a criminal offence?
Yes ___ No ___

Are there currently any outstanding criminal charges against you?
Yes ___ No ___

Note that a criminal charge or conviction will not automatically exclude you from employment or volunteer opportunities. The nature of the employment or volunteer activities and the circumstances related to the charge or conviction will be considered.

Do you know of any reason why you should not participate as an employee or volunteer where you will be in contact with children?
Yes ___ No ___

If you answered YES to any of these questions, please provide details below. *We will keep this information confidential.* Please provide the name, position, and telephone number of at least one authority with whom we may discuss matters and confirm details.

☐ I certify that the information given in this form is true and correct, and I understand that falsification or omission of required information may result in my removal from the program. To ensure the safety and well-being of children, I hereby grant permission for the program manager to conduct any investigation, including a criminal-record search, that s/he may think desirable in light of the information I have provided on this form.

Print name   Signature of volunteer or employee   Date

☐ I have witnessed this signature.

Print name   Signature of program coordinator   Date

Paid or Volunteer Employment Agreement

Use this template to create your own customized employment or volunteer agreement.

Have each paid or volunteer staff member sign this agreement. Provide him or her with a copy of the signed agreement.

Keep all of the original signed agreements in your confidential personnel binder.

[DATE]

This letter certifies that [NAME OF EMPLOYEE OR VOLUNTEER] has accepted the [VOLUNTEER OR PAID] position of [TITLE OF POSITION] with [NAME OF MEAL PROGRAM].

TERMS OF EMPLOYMENT

The place of work is [ADDRESS OF MEAL PROGRAM].

[NAME OF EMPLOYEE OR VOLUNTEER] will begin work on [DATE]. This is a [PERMANENT OR TEMPORARY] position [THAT IS EXPECTED TO END ON (DATE)].

[NAME OF EMPLOYEE OR VOLUNTEER] is expected to work approximately [NUMBER] hours a week, at the following days and times:

- [DAY] [TIME]
- [DAY] [TIME]
- [DAY] [TIME]

DUTIES AND RESPONSIBILITIES

[NAME OF EMPLOYEE OR VOLUNTEER] is expected to perform the following duties:

- [DUTY 1]
- [DUTY 2]
- [DUTY 3]

S/he will be responsible for the following:

- [RESPONSIBILITY 1]
- [RESPONSIBILITY 2]
- [RESPONSIBILITY 3]

S/he will NOT be responsible for the following

- [ITEM 1]
- [ITEM 2]
- [ITEM 3]

REMUNERATION AND VACATION ENTITLEMENT

This is a [PAID OR VOLUNTEER] position.

The remuneration is [AMOUNT PER HOUR, MONTH, OR YEAR].

[NAME OF EMPLOYEE OR VOLUNTEER] is entitled to [NUMBER] weeks of vacation per year.

EQUIPMENT AND SUPPLIES

All meal ingredients, kitchen supplies, [AND PROTECTIVE CLOTHING] are provided by [NAME OF MEAL PROGRAM].

[NAME OF EMPLOYEE OR VOLUNTEER] is required to supply [ITEM(S)] and [HIS OR HER OWN PROTECTIVE CLOTHING]. S/he is expected to wear [ITEM(S)] while on duty.

SIGNATURES AND CONTACT INFORMATION

☐ We agree to the aforementioned terms and conditions.

_____

Print name   Signature of volunteer or employee   Date

_____

Address

_____

Home phone   Mobile phone   Email address

_____

Print name   Signature of program coordinator   Date

Code of Conduct and Confidentiality Agreement

You can customize this agreement to meet the specific needs of your program.

Have each paid or volunteer staff member sign this confidentiality agreement. Provide him or her with a copy of the signed agreement.

Keep all of the original signed agreements in your confidential personnel binder.

VOLUNTEER CODE OF CONDUCT AND CONFIDENTIALITY AGREEMENT

Thank you for your time and commitment to helping us. We all benefit greatly from your efforts.

It's important that all volunteers in our program act as positive, supportive role models. Please read the following guidelines to positive behaviour, and indicate with your signature that you agree to abide by them.

As a volunteer with our program, you are expected to do all of the following:

- Treat clients and staff with respect
- Act as a positive role model for clients, staff, and community members
- Keep the personal information of all clients and staff—including anything you may see and hear during your volunteer activities—strictly confidential
- Carry out your duties in a reliable, timely manner
- Obtain the program director's approval before initiating any new procedures or activities
- Notify the program director of any change in your availability
- Comply with all program policies
- Promote community volunteerism in a professional manner

You must also ensure that all clients:

- Understand and follow the program's rules
- Interact with one another in a respectful manner
- Understand that any form of abuse will be not tolerated and will be cause for immediate removal

Our clients' safety is of paramount importance. As a volunteer, you are in a position of trust. It is essential that you help safeguard our clients' physical and emotional safety.

You are not permitted to use drugs or alcohol on the facility's premises, nor to sell drugs or alcohol to any client.

If you compromise a client's safety, we will immediately revoke your volunteer status.

You are not permitted to discuss, access, review, disclose, or use confidential client or staff information unless required by law to do so.

We greatly appreciate your continuing efforts and assistance as a volunteer. Thank you for your support. We look forward to working with you.

☐ I have read and understand the above statements and agree to comply with the rules and expectations set out in this Code of Conduct. I understand that failure to comply with the Code of Conduct may result in my removal as a volunteer.

_____

Print name   Signature of volunteer or employee   Date

☐ I have witnessed this signature.

_____

Print name   Signature of program coordinator   Date

Sign-In Sheet

Keep this form in your procedures binder. Ensure that all of your paid and volunteer staff sign in and out for every shift.

VOLUNTEERS, PLEASE SIGN IN AND OUT

Date	Name	Time In	Time Out

Sample Letter Asking for Equipment Donations

Following is an example of the kind of letter you can use to ask local organizations and businesses to donate equipment for your program.

Customize it to suit the needs of your particular program.

Dear [RECIPIENT]:

My name is [NAME]. I am [POSITION] with [NAME OF PROGRAM].

Too many people these days don't have enough to eat.

You may be surprised to learn that families who look like they're doing just fine may be secretly experiencing hunger and privation. It's a hidden epidemic within our community . . . and it's not their fault. No matter how hard they work, some people are just unlucky. They may become injured, or lose their jobs, or lose their usual support networks, or any number of things.

[NAME OF PROGRAM] is responding by supplying healthy food to people who need it.

Here are some facts about our program.

- Our clients are [AGE RANGE].
- They live in [AREA].
- We operate our program in [NAME OF FACILITY AND DAYS OF SERVICE].
- Our clients' circumstances are [OUTLINE NEEDS].

[INCLUDE SOME RELEVANT STATISTICS. Those for children who eat breakfast versus those who go without breakfast, for example, are alarming. Kids who eat school breakfasts attend school for an average of 1.5 more days per week than their meal-skipping peers, and their math scores are approximately 17.5 percent higher. These students with increased attendance and scores are 20 percent more likely to graduate from high school. High school graduates earn, on average, $10,090 more per year than their non-diploma-holding counterparts and are significantly less likely to experience hunger in adulthood.]

How can you help?

Could you help by providing some of the items we need to get started? If so, we'd be grateful to receive any of the following:

- [ITEM 1]
- [ITEM 2]
- [ITEM 3]
- [ITEM 4]

Please let me know how you can help.

We'll think of you and your donation every time we use it, every time we see a [CHILD OR CLIENT] leave the table with a full tummy and a smile, and every time we ease the heart of someone who is struggling hard yet still in need.

Each time we make a difference, your donation will make all the difference. Please help give our program a solid foundation on which to flourish.

On behalf of the people in our community who are at risk, and on behalf of those who are trying to help them, thank you.

[NAME]
[POSITION]
[NAME OF PROGRAM]
[PHONE NUMBER]
[EMAIL ADDRESS]

Client Log Sheet

Use the following form to keep a count of your clients. You'll need this information for planning and ordering. You may need it for funding applications, too.

Keep the client log sheet in your procedures binder. Ensure that all of your paid and volunteer staff are familiar with it.

You might want to assign the task of keeping this log every day to a specific person.

CLIENT LOG SHEET

Date	Number of Meals Served	Notes

Acknowledgements

I would like to give my greatest appreciation to my husband, Steve, and our four sons, Taylor, Kyle, Chayden and Conner; I love you with my whole heart.

My mom, Sherry, dad, Ken, and brother, Daniel; your support and love in my life has always pushed me forward.

The support of my mother- and father-in-law, my aunts, uncles, siblings-in-law, cousins, nieces, nephews and friends; muah!

My incredibly skilled editor, Anne, for the passion and time we both shared in making this book. You do truly have the most giving and generous heart.

Greg, Cheryl, Jonathan, Toby, Heather and all at Iguana Books; for believing in this book from day one, for the amazing way you brought my book cover idea to life and for the final editing.

Sue Mercer, Sue Hildebrandt, Adam Henry, Deb Page, Maria Shannon, Shelley Coburn, Tony Mitchell, Jen Verbeek and Susan Cairns; so all of your hard work does not go unnoticed.

And to all of the people running these food programs or braving the first steps of developing one, this has an immeasurable impact on your communities. You may never know to whom or how far your dedication will reach, only that all of your efforts will grow further than you will ever know.

www.ingramcontent.com/pod-product-compliance
Lightning Source LLC
Chambersburg PA
CBHW051436270326
41935CB00031B/1832